Ornament
OF
Grace
and other stories for girls

I enjoy sharing my books as I do my friends, asking only that you treat them well and see them safely home.

© 2018 by TGS International, a wholly owned subsidiary of Christian Aid Ministries, Berlin, Ohio.

All rights reserved. No part of this book may be used, reproduced, or stored in any retrieval system, in any form or by any means, electronic or mechanical, without written permission from the publisher except for brief quotations embodied in critical articles and reviews.

ISBN: 978-1-947319-38-7

Cover and text layout design: Kristi Yoder

Printed in the USA

Published by:

TGS International
P.O. Box 355
Berlin, Ohio 44610 USA
Phone: 330.893.4828
Fax: 330.893.2305
www.tgsinternational.com

TGS001640

Ornament OF Grace
and other stories for girls

CHRISTINE DILLER

Table of Contents

Author's Note vii
Dedication ix
1) Ornament of Grace 11
2) They're My Family 17
3) Just Two Neighbor Ladies 23
4) Maggie and the Peas 29
5) The Wounds of a Friend 39
6) We Want Risa 45
7) Words in Her Mouth 51
8) One-of-a-Kind Girl 57
9) Parakeet Friend 63
10) A Monster in the House 69
11) A Little Tongue 75
12) Give Some, Save Some, Spend Some 81
13) Only a Thistle 87

14)	Strict Mom	91
15)	Plenty of Time	97
16)	The Treasure Box	103
17)	Annette and a Pair of Shoes	109
18)	Only for Fun	115
19)	It's the Love That Matters	121
20)	Against the Darkness	127
	About the Author	133

Author's Note

This is a compilation of true-to-life stories. "Words in Her Mouth" and "Against the Darkness" are my own actual experiences. Many of the other stories "sprouted" from the seed of a true happening or a lesson learned in my own life or in the lives of my family. I have fictionalized the characters and settings around that seed taken from real-life happenings.

Dedication

I dedicate this book to you, my four wonderful daughters. You are gifts from God. You have taught me so much and have made my experience as a mother beautiful.

- To Mary, who inspires me to write by writing also
- To Analise, who encourages me to fulfill my dreams
- To Dora, who wants to see me happy and is always ready to help me in any way she can
- To Betsy, my youngest daughter, who did a lot of the housework while I was writing

1
Ornament of Grace

Grace was the kind of girl you'd never look at twice in a crowd, yet I can still see her walk calmly as though assured that all is right with her world or that all will be right someday. Grace wasn't beautiful, but something about her was unforgettably pretty.

While some of the other girls' hair drooped alarmingly in front of their veils, Grace's curly light brown hair was combed back simply. Her clothes were simpler and plainer than ours, but there was nothing unpleasant about her appearance. She dressed neatly and attractively.

I hear again her soft voice that first time I went to a youth gathering.

"How are you today?" she said. "I'm glad you started coming to youth group."

I smiled back at her. It would have been hard not to. Her

charming, contagious smile made me feel warm and welcome.

The youth girls chattered as youth girls do.

"Those old sweaters everyone used to wear are soooo . . . gross," complained one girl.

"I know," agreed another. "I was glad when Mom finally got me one that fits better like yours. I told her everyone is wearing these now, so she got one for me." I glanced around. It was just as I'd thought. Not everyone wore the newer, tighter style of sweater.

Grace wore a straight gray sweater all the time. It was exactly the kind of sweater the girls called disgusting, but she never seemed to hear conversations like these. She'd calmly listen to the girls talk for a minute; then she'd speak quietly to someone who was often unnoticed in the group.

Grace always wore what the other girls called "Grandma prints." You'd think she wouldn't have any friends, but she did. She liked everybody and was friendly to everyone, even to those girls who said her sweater was gross and her dresses grandma-ish. She just didn't seem to pay any attention to their talk.

I was getting more and more intrigued with Grace. When she invited me to her place overnight, I was eager to go.

Her father met me at the door. He was slim and erect, his thinning brown hair perfectly in place as always. His checkered shirt and work pants gave him a different look than when I saw him at church.

Shaking my hand warmly, he said, "I'm glad Grace has you for a friend. You're very welcome at our house. Grace gets lonely here with just me."

At the table, he passed the roast beef and mashed potatoes to me first. I wasn't used to a table set just for three and I the only honored guest. It felt strange. After a dessert of Jell-O with fruit and oatmeal cookies, he left us and went to sit in the living room to read.

As we cleaned up the kitchen, Grace confided, "That was Father's favorite supper. I wanted to have pizza and ice cream for you, but Father wanted to have something better than 'that cardboard with tomato sauce and cheese on it.' And ice cream gives him indigestion." She chuckled a little.

"That's okay," I said honestly. "Supper was very good."

When we joined her father in the living room, Grace showed me pictures of her family. There were four brothers with a little curly-headed Grace. I looked carefully at the pictures of the mother whom I didn't remember. She was short and rather plump in some of the pictures. I decided Grace looked like her father. Grace put the pictures back on the doily on the table. A lamp with a white glass globe shared the doily. It had flowers painted on it. Glass mottoes painted with flowers and Bible verses hung nearby. It reminded me of my grandparents' living room.

Later, when we were in Grace's room, I said, "I want to go to Bible school next year when I'm finished with school. My sister went. She made new friends and learned a lot more about the Bible."

"I'd like to go too," Grace answered. "But I don't think I will. Father doesn't want me to. I guess he thinks he can't do without me. I'm all he has anymore. Mother's been gone five years, and all of my brothers are married. He needs me,

I guess." She looked at her toe tracing the pattern on the rug. After a pause, she looked up at me and smiled. "But I'm glad I can be here and do things for him. It's not really hard keeping him happy. When he's happy, I'm happy." Behind her smile, her eyes sparkled with tears. Somehow I felt the tears weren't so much tears of grief as they were tears of love.

We talked on, and I began girl talk about clothes.

"Mom wants to take me shopping for some dress fabric. Maybe you could go along."

"I would like that," she said. "I think Dad could spare me for a day."

"I want to get some of that new fabric," I continued. "It's supposed to be soft to wear, and I think they have such pretty colors in it."

I stopped chattering long enough to look at Grace. Her head was down and her fingers pleated the bedspread. Something was wrong.

"Maybe you could get one too," I said. "I'll buy it for you. We'll have matching dresses."

"I don't know if my father would like the new material," she said.

Oh, no, I groaned inwardly. *What have I done now?* It was true that her dress fabrics were always of the older patterns and styles. But why shouldn't she have something new too?

"Maybe he would get used to it if we got one," I suggested. "Do you think he would mind too much?"

"Father is kind and loving to me," she began. "He buys me presents sometimes for no reason, but he is happiest when I like what he likes. He feels bad when he thinks I like the things of the world too much. To him, new things are of the world."

"But I thought he liked me, and my clothes are newer styles," I said, glancing at my colorful sneakers and her plain ones.

"He can overlook things like that in others," she said, "but in me he can't."

"But these things aren't things of the world," I protested. "They are just newer. My mom fusses about immodesty and bright colors, and I have to admit that what she says is true, but new can be okay. She just always says she has to give it some thought and talk it over with Dad."

"Well," said Grace, "I think your parents are wise. I can see you don't just have what others have and do what others do. Yet it . . . well . . . you've said it, really. Sometimes new is okay, but Dad loves me so, and he loves the Lord so. This is his way, and I just can't hurt him."

After that night I understood Grace. We became close friends. I never worried that the rest of the youth group would shun me because of my friendship with her. Grace was respected by all the youth.

No, sometimes they didn't invite her. And yes, sometimes they went around a corner to finish talking when she appeared, but never did they make fun of her. They all liked her. It was impossible not to. It was her kind ways to everyone.

"We're glad to have you," she said again and again to newcomers.

"How is school going?" she'd ask one of the younger ones.

"Do you like your new job?" she asked another.

"How is your grandma doing?" she'd remember to ask when

the rest of us had forgotten that someone's grandmother was sick.

She was always ready to help work. While the rest of us giggled and forgot there was work to do, Grace cheerfully asked the youth leaders what she could do next.

So it was, fifteen years later, after I had married and moved away from Grace, I remembered her when I read in Proverbs 1:8 and 9 that honoring your father is like an ornament of grace for your head. Yes, I remembered Grace because her name is in that verse, but even more because I recalled her devotion and obedience to her father in things that seemed to us teenagers as unnecessary for Christian living. I remembered how outstanding she was in taking her quiet, unashamed stand. Those verses said it all. She was unforgettably pretty because she was wearing the King's ornament of grace.

> My son, hear the instruction of thy father, and
> forsake not the law of thy mother: For they shall
> be an ornament of grace unto thy head, and
> chains about thy neck.
> Proverbs 1:8–9

2
They're My Family

"Aren't there enough children in your family? Don't you think another one is too many?"

Julie stopped snapping car seat buckles. Who was talking? She turned to see her friend Allison.

Julie was confused. She didn't know what to say.

"Don't you get tired of helping to take care of them?" Allison asked.

"Not too much," answered Julie. "I like them all."

Julie turned back to her task of making sure her two young siblings were securely in their car seats. She was helping Dad with the children at church this morning. Mom was at home with their new baby, Etta. Baby Etta was the seventh child in their family and such a dear! What was Allison saying? Would she really think their baby was "too many" when she saw her?

Allison was gone when Julie turned around, and Julie was

glad. She was relieved when Dad appeared with six-year-old Zach. They drove around the church to find twelve-year-old Seth and nine-year-old Jake. Then they headed home. Julie was subdued even though two-year-old Leah tugged at her sleeve to ask questions and four-year-old Sara hummed a new song. Julie's thoughts were going around like the wheels on the van. *Did Allison say what others thought too? Did others think that baby Etta was "too many"?*

At home, around the long kitchen table, Julie had to admit there was a lot of noise. Finally Dad subdued the chatter. "Not so noisy, children. Why, you'll wake your baby sister."

They stayed home the rest of the day and played games in the evening. Once again the house was full of happy noise.

On Monday, Julie could have thought there were too many in her family by the piles of dirty clothing the family dumped on the floor by the washing machine before breakfast. Julie fried eggs and made toast. It would be foolish to wait for Mom to make breakfast. Mom had the baby to take care of first.

It was Seth's turn to wash the dishes. Julie sorted wash, and soon the hum of the busy washing machine filled the house. Most of the children had schoolwork to do and scattered to their bedrooms to work. Julie brought her math to the kitchen table so she could refill the washer when it finished.

"May I hold Etta?" she asked Mom.

"You can't do schoolwork very well holding a baby," protested Mom.

"Oh, yes I can. Let me try," she begged.

"Okay, you may try it," said Mom. "She is very dear when she is so small."

"That's it," commented Julie. "She'll grow up fast." She kissed the soft hair tufted on Etta's head as she held the warm little bundle. "I'll do good work," she promised. Mom helped Seth with his math and kept an eye on Zach and Jake's progress with their books.

Between hanging out wash and helping Leah and Sara hold the baby, Julie really didn't get a lot of math done, but she didn't mind today. Etta was so precious. She certainly wasn't "too many" today.

After lunch the younger children and Mom took naps. Seth and Jake went out to ride their bicycles. Julie got a lot of school work done.

The sunny day had dried the laundry well. The boys helped Julie bring it in; then she folded it, and each child put his or her own clothing away. Aunt Lena brought supper, and soon Dad was home. He volunteered to wash the supper dishes. Julie finished her schoolwork and then went to bed, a tired but contented girl. She loved her family. They made her life so full and complete.

The whole week was busy with the care of her brothers and sisters as Mom recuperated, but Julie didn't worry about it. That is, she didn't worry until Sunday morning when she was helping to dress the small ones.

What were the ladies at church going to say? Would they think Baby Etta is "too many"?

Allison sat beside Julie in church. Julie gave her a small smile. She didn't feel like talking to her friend. After church, she slipped out the back, but not soon enough to miss seeing the cluster of women around Mom. They were admiring the new baby, but how many of them were secretly thinking "too many"? She didn't want to watch.

On her way to the van, Zach stopped her. He was flanked by two boys with smiles and eyes as twinkly as his. "We found a toad," he said. "Do you want to see it?" Julie admired the toad. She also admired the three smiles. Little boys were fun and made life exciting. How could any of them be "too many"?

"You'd better let the toad go now," she advised the boys, turning toward the van.

"Julie," another voice waylaid her, "wait a minute."

Julie tuned to see Sister Ruth coming. "How are you?" Ruth asked with her wide, cheerful grin. "How is your mom and the new baby?" Ruth didn't wait for an answer as she bubbled on. "I was the oldest girl in my family of seven. I liked it. Do you?" She stopped for an answer this time, and her brown eyes looked kindly at Julie.

Julie answered slowly, "Yes, I guess so."

Ruth came closer and stopped smiling. "Is something wrong?"

"Not really. It's just that other people—" Julie stopped, not knowing what else to say.

"Other people," repeated Ruth. "Let me guess. Other people think big sisters work hard and don't like to be the big sister."

"I guess," Julie shrugged.

"Here's my advice," said Ruth. "A big sister does work hard, but all those younger brothers and sisters think she's pretty special too, don't they?"

Julie smiled. "Yes, they do."

"Then don't worry about those 'others.' They don't understand." She went to get into the car her husband had brought around.

Julie had reached the van this time when a breathless "Julie!" stopped her again.

Julie remained turned away. It was Allison. Julie didn't want to talk to her right now.

"Julie, listen," said Allison. "I'm sorry for what I said. It was very, very rude. I didn't think before I said it." Her voice trembled. She stopped and swallowed, then went on. "I get lonely at home. My sister and two brothers have jobs and go away a lot with friends. I often complain to Mom because I wish I had some little brothers and sisters. She tries to make me content with the family God has given us. She tries to tell me I might get tired of helping with them. I really wanted to know if that is how you feel with all your little brothers and sisters."

Julie turned to face her friend. "Sometimes I do," she admitted honestly. "I could use more peace and quiet sometimes, but I wouldn't want to do without any of my brothers and sisters either. They're my family. Most of the time I don't mind helping with the work."

"I'd love to help," offered Allison. "Do you think I could come over sometime when you have to babysit?"

"Sure," said Julie. "Sara and Leah would love that."

A few minutes later Julie and her family were leaving the church lot in their big family van. Allison was watching. She waved, and Julie waved back. Julie was happy with her family. She knew Allison was happy with hers too, even though she was lonely at times. Julie was glad they understood each other now. She looked forward to sharing her brothers and sisters with Allison.

3
Just Two Neighbor Ladies

They were just two neighbor ladies until Janet learned their story. They lived in a small stone-fronted house with fluffy white curtains in the dormer windows. When they asked Janet's brother to mow their lawn, Janet's family began to know them better. One sister, Mina, was having health problems. The other sister, Molly, was healthy but struggled more and more with the care of her sister.

It wasn't long until Molly called and asked if someone would help with the housework too. Janet readily agreed to come. She'd been looking for a part-time job close to home, and working for the sisters sounded exciting.

"It's a lovely morning, isn't it?" Molly greeted Janet at the door on her first morning at work. She wore a simple lavender house dress. Her white hair was pinned up in a twist on the back of her head. Bright blue eyes twinkled when she smiled. Janet felt at home with her immediately.

"How's your family?" she asked. "You have a busy household over there."

"I guess we do," Janet answered, thinking of her two older siblings coming and going to jobs and youth activities.

"There is always someone or something moving in your yard," Molly said.

That must be my two younger brothers and their dogs, thought Janet.

"I enjoy watching them," Molly continued. "I like families. But come now and I'll show you what I want you to do. I just can't keep up with everything here anymore. I'm so glad you can help me. I wouldn't want to hire just anybody.

"First I want you to dust, and then hang out some wash. I like the smell that comes in on line-dried clothes, but I'm just getting too old and stiff to do it much anymore. We'll have to wait to run the vacuum sweeper until my sister, Mina, gets up. She likes to sleep a little later."

Janet was soon done with the dusting and the load of laundry. She wondered what she would do if Mina didn't get up soon. Just then a woman in a silky housecoat appeared in the doorway.

"Where's Molly?" the woman asked in an abrupt manner. Then looking at Janet the second time, she added, "When you clean my room, don't move my things around. I don't like my things moved."

"Okay," answered Janet. She studied the woman who must be Mina more closely. Her hair was curly and brown. It didn't go with the wrinkles on her face. Her eyes met Janet's for only a moment. Then she looked away.

"Where is Molly?" she asked again. Then as Molly appeared, she said in the tone of a fretful child, "I'm ready for breakfast now."

"Good morning," said Molly cheerfully. "What would you like for breakfast this morning?"

"Whatever," Mina mumbled, shrugging impatiently. "You know what I like."

"Sure," said Molly. "Did you sleep well last night?"

Mina laughed shortly. "You know I never sleep well. I don't know why those pills the doctor gave me don't work. Don't make eggs," she ordered when she saw Molly get an egg box out of the refrigerator. "Cream of wheat would be better."

Molly put the eggs away without comment and turned to the cupboard. Janet left the kitchen to get the vacuuming done. She wondered if Mina was always this grouchy.

Janet enjoyed working for Molly. She looked forward to talking with her. They talked about the houseplants and flowers she grew around the house. Molly gave cuttings to Janet to start her own collection. Molly often asked about Janet's family.

"You have such a nice family," she said more than once.

Janet didn't work there long before she found out Mina seemed hard to please all of the time. The sisters were so different; it was hard to imagine they were sisters.

One day Mina scolded, "It's no wonder I can't find anything. You know I always want you to put my magazines on this table. When you lay them just any old place, I can't find them. Next time you get the mail, lay all of mine here." She slapped the table with her hand.

And then another day Janet heard, "Did you get that spot out of my blouse yet? You know that's my favorite. Take it to the cleaners or whatever you have to do. I have to have that blouse spotless."

Molly said little in reply to these accusations. She would sometimes seem extra quiet for a bit after being scolded, but soon she would be smiling her sunny smile again.

When Janet cleaned, she dusted a bureau with old photographs on it. One was of two small girls. Another was of a family—father, mother, one boy, and two girls. One day Janet asked Molly about them. Molly said they were pictures of herself and her family.

Janet examined those pictures every week. The two girls wore matching dresses with low waists and a ruffle of lace down the front of each. One had long sausage curls hanging over her shoulders. She was smiling a confident smile. The other girl's face was narrow and her hair was cut in a short, bobbed fashion just below her ears. Both girls had big bows in their hair. The girl with short hair had a shy half smile. They didn't look as much alike as sisters might. Janet couldn't tell which was Molly and which was Mina.

She carried the family picture to Molly. "Which one are you?" she asked.

"Oh, my," Molly chuckled, "We never looked alike, Mina and I. Mina had the curls, and I was always thin and pale."

Janet looked wonderingly at the Molly of today and back at the picture. Maybe the narrow-faced girl did have Molly's nose and chin, but Molly's face now shone beneath her white hair. Janet would have thought she once had been very pretty. The picture of the smiling, curly-headed girl didn't look much like the wrinkled face of Mina either.

"I couldn't tell which was which," Janet said.

"Well," Molly said, "Mina was always such a cute girl. Everywhere she went people commented how cute she was." She chuckled. "And me . . . well, they would look at me and have nothing to say. There never was anything good to say about my looks.

"But it's all right," she added. "Pretty is as pretty does, isn't it?" She looked questioningly at Janet.

"Yes," Janet answered.

"At least that's what my grandma always said." Molly patted Janet's arm and laughed merrily. Then she sobered. "It took me a long time to learn that, though. For years, the fact that my sister was pretty and I wasn't got me down. My parents used to talk about her nice looks and how boys would want to marry her. 'Molly, now,' they would add, 'will never marry. She'll always stay with us and care for us.'

"I didn't stay with them at first. I left home for college and got a degree in education. I taught for five years, and then Mother got cancer. I had to come home to care for her because no one else was available. My brother couldn't leave his job to move because of his family, and Mina wasn't capable. Mother lived only six more months. Then Dad wanted me to stay with him, so I did.

"Mina? Well, Mina married and divorced before she had a chance to grow up. Then she remarried, and that husband cheated on her. When she married the third time, she seemed to settle down somewhat. Her husband was older than her and waited on her hand and foot. Then he died suddenly of a heart attack. She moved back in with Dad and me. Later Dad died, and just recently my brother died also, so there's just the two of us left. Mina is the only family I have left.

I've learned to accept my life and make the best of it. I wish Mina could do that too. She is so unhappy, and I feel sorry for her. I try to help her all I can."

A few weeks after this conversation, Janet walked in the door as the sisters were finishing lunch. Molly told Janet to sit down and sample a cake she had made. Janet had eaten a quick lunch so she would arrive on time. She thought she had room for cake. She sat at the table with them to eat. Bright afternoon sun streamed into the kitchen. It revealed the two sisters unmercifully. Mina's "young" hair was in place as usual, but her heavy makeup didn't cover her wrinkles. Her red lips stood out startlingly. Her voice was querulous and demanding. She looked old and cross.

Molly's face was wrinkled too, but her eyes shone with contentment as she smiled across the table at Janet. Her voice was definitely the frail voice of an old lady, but her words were friendly and sweet.

And that is the history of two neighbor ladies whom Janet learned to know. One had started life with a pretty face and was ending it with the ugliness of self and discontent. The other had started with a plain face and came to her sunset years with a beautiful countenance that radiated love and joy.

The beauty of one young girl had deceived those around her and because of that she had never learned to value inner beauty of character.

Favor is deceitful and beauty is vain. Proverbs 31:30

4

Maggie
and the Peas

Grandpa's blue-as-the-sky eyes twinkled at Diane.

She grinned back.

He winked!

Happy relief replaced the worry that had been on Diane's mind for most of a week. Grandpa had gone to the hospital for knee surgery, and then further complications had developed. He hadn't opened his eyes completely for days, and the family had all been worried.

Today he was lying there in the hospital bed with a needle in his arm and an oxygen tube in his nose. The antiseptic smell of the hospital enveloped them, but Grandpa had smiled and even winked at her. He would get better.

Diane didn't know what she would do without her grandpa. She had started going with the youth and was trying to fit in, but it felt like Mom and Dad wanted her to be the biggest oddball ever. It seemed they were always bugging her about something. She wasn't allowed to wear this and that. She had to be home at a certain time. Sometimes she wasn't even allowed to go to certain activities. She couldn't see the need for all the fuss and wondered why she couldn't do what was all right for others in her church. Diane couldn't understand, but she could count on Grandpa to cheer her up with his jokes and his twinkling eyes.

So she was especially glad to see him doing much better. Grandpa did so well that he was home from the hospital the next day.

Grandma called and asked, "Can you come over soon? Grandpa wants to talk to you about his goats." Diane didn't know why Grandpa wanted to talk to her about goats, but she wanted to see Grandpa.

Mom dropped Diane off at Grandpa's house after school. Diane ran in the lane.

"Hi, Grandma," Diane said when Grandma opened the door. "How's Grandpa?"

"He's in here," she said. "He's not as well as he'd like to be, but I've been telling him he's a fortunate man to be home."

Grandpa was sitting in the recliner. He raised his hand. "Howdy," he said. "I'm home, but I can't do anything. I can't even walk out and look at my goats, much less milk them."

"I went out and checked them," said Grandma. "They're fine."

"But you can't milk them," said Grandpa.

"No, I can't," admitted Grandma. "My hands are stiff with arthritis, but Sam is doing a good job."

"Maybe, maybe not," grumbled Grandpa. "All he thinks about is getting done and getting his money. That's what I wanted to talk to you about." He frowned at Diane.

Diane wasn't worried. She was used to his frowns. She knew he was still thinking of Sam's quickness at chore time and not about her.

He kept frowning. "Do you think you could take care of those pesky goats until I'm allowed to go out again? Do you think you can keep them out of your grandma's garden? She's got peas blooming, and those critters do love peas. It takes a lot of know-how with fences to keep them in when there are peas to eat."

"I don't know anything about fences," Diane answered honestly, "but I would like to learn to milk the goats."

"Well," said Grandpa, "I guess you'll have to do. It looks like I don't have any choice. What will you charge me? I guess you'll want more than that boy does."

"Grandpa, I don't need any money to help you. You're going to need your money to pay the hospital bill."

"Done," he said. "I'll tell Sam not to come tonight. When your father gets home from work, he can come along over here and show you how it's done."

The goats were baa-ing for their feed by the time she and Dad got there. Dad milked a brown goat while Diane milked a white one. At first she squeezed the teats just like Dad did, but nothing happened. She kept trying until suddenly milk streamed out. Diane grinned. Milking was going to be fun. The goat was very good. She stood there chewing her cud as if Diane did this every day.

The next day was Saturday. Diane went over to do the chores herself. Dolly, the big white one she'd learned to milk first, came over for a head rub. Diane rubbed her between the knobby bumps of horns on her head and then scratched under her neck. Dolly was glad to see her. Diane milked her without any problems other than her hands got tired.

The smaller goat was brown with large white spots. Her name was Sadie. She came to greet Diane too, but she didn't let Diane touch her until she put grain in the feed box. As soon as Sadie put her head through the bars to eat it, Diane quickly fastened the head lock. Sadie was in position to be milked, but their problems weren't over. Diane touched her; Sadie kicked. Diane tried talking nicely to her. She petted her a little. Sadie kept chewing but tried to peer around the bars at Diane to see who she was and what she would do.

Gingerly Diane started milking. The pail started to fill up. Diane relaxed and began to find her rhythm. Wham! Out went Sadie's hoof and over went the pail. White milk poured out and down through the boards in the milking stand. Diane yanked the bucket back and stood there looking angrily at Sadie.

Sadie turned her head as far as she could to look at Diane. "What happened?" she seemed to ask. Diane felt like whamming her but controlled herself and finished milking Sadie. She stood placidly now and let Diane put a half inch of milk in the pail.

When Diane took the pail of milk to Grandma, Grandma simply said, "Sometimes that happens to Grandpa too. Sadie is hard to milk." Diane watched her strain the milk.

"What about the fences, Grandma? Grandpa was worried about the fences more than anything else."

"I'll come out and show you what to watch for before you go home," she said after placing the milk jar in the refrigerator.

Back outside, Diane got an introduction to the remaining four goats and some kids. Maggie was black with some white on her feet and back. The remaining three were white and she couldn't tell them apart.

"Grandpa has a board fence on this side close to the house and garden," Grandma pointed out. "It's the best for keeping the goats in because it doesn't sag when they put their feet on it; however, the boards do come loose. Sometimes the goats rub the fence to scratch their backs, loosening the boards. Sometimes the kids scoot underneath if the ground wears away. So watch for loose boards and gaps under the fence. Use the hammer and nails in the tool shed to fasten loose boards again."

They walked around the corner of the fence. "This section of fence is woven wire," explained Grandma. "The goats put their feet on it too to reach those tree branches. After they do that for a while, the fence sags and they can jump over it. Your job is to look for sagging fence and pull it up. They also put their heads under this fence to reach grass and weeds on the other side. This can make a hole to crawl through. You can't be here all day to watch and make sure the goats are in, but when you check the fence every evening, you can fix the problems. Then I'll just have to keep an eye on them in the daytime."

That sounded easy enough to Diane, but the next night

Grandma said, "Maggie and Dina were out today. I had to get them in. They came trotting up the lane, so I had time to get them in before they got into the garden. Take a close look at the woven wire along the lane."

Diane went out and circled the pasture, looking for a possible escape route, but she found nothing.

She reported to Grandma who said, "It's hard to find their holes. I'll go out and look around some more. I can't go the whole way around, but I'll look as far as I can."

When Diane hurried in the lane the next day, Maggie was in the garden again. She lifted her head. The last of a pea vine disappeared down her throat as she stood there calmly looking at Diane. Diane yelled and ran. Sedately, Maggie turned, walked a little ahead of her, and waited at the gate, turning to look at her again as if to say, "What's all the fuss? I'll go back in like a good goat."

Diane felt bad about the pea vine. She didn't want to tell Grandma, but she had to ask her to come out and look at the fence.

"Don't feel too bad," Grandma said. "Goats can be very hard to keep in."

"But Grandpa will get someone else to take care of the goats."

"I don't think he will," said Grandma. "I don't know who else he would get, and the goats get out for him sometimes too." They looked all along the fence. Grandma found a spot where the ground was worn away under the fence. "Maggie is a big goat," she said. "I don't know how she could get out here, but you never know with Maggie."

Diane put some big rocks in that hole like Grandma told her to, but Maggie was out the next day, and the next. Soon the peas were all eaten back to the ground. Diane stood there looking at the small green stubs of plants that were left.

Grandma came up beside her and slipped her arm around her. "Don't worry," she said. "It's not the first time I lost all my peas to goats. You did your best."

"But what did Grandpa say?" Diane asked

She squeezed Diane closer to her. "I didn't tell him," she said. "Sometime the time will be right for you to tell him yourself."

Maggie behaved better after the peas were all eaten. Diane milked the goats for another week before Grandpa came out to see his goats. They were glad to see him. They crowded along the fence. Maggie put her feet on a board and reached out to nibble Grandpa's cap.

"That goat," he said as he grabbed for his cap. "Many are the times I've thought about selling her. I don't know why I don't."

"She's a bad goat," Diane said. "She wouldn't stay in until she ate all of Grandma's peas."

"Oh? Grandma didn't tell me that."

Diane blushed. "She told me I could tell you myself."

"Well, so now you tell me. But since it's confession time, I guess I'll have to confess she gets out for me too."

Grandpa was quiet a moment, watching his goats. Then he said, "Goats have their own personalities. I guess you've noticed that."

"Yes," Diane said. "Dolly is a good goat. I never have any trouble with her. Sadie was very hard to milk. When she did let me milk her, she spilled the milk."

"Sadie doesn't like strangers," Grandpa said. "She wants the same person to take care of her all the time, but that's not always possible.

"I often think those goats are a lot like dissatisfied people," continued Grandpa. "Watch them now that we're not paying any attention to them. See how they move around as they eat. They take a bite here and a bite there. There's plenty of grass everywhere in that pasture, but they keep looking for something different. Look at Maggie."

Maggie had her hoofs planted daintily on the wire fence, making it sag. She was reaching her knobby head out for the nearby tree branches. Her long tongue reached and reached but couldn't quite get a bite. Diane laughed. Maggie looked around at them and dropped to the ground.

"Now watch her," said Grandpa. "See what else she does."

Soon Maggie was down on her knees reaching her head under the fence to try to get a weed growing there.

"There is luscious green grass growing right under her feet," said Grandpa, "but she wants something different. Isn't that like some people we know?"

"Who?" Diane asked. She was puzzled.

"We've been concerned, your dad and I," began Grandpa, "about the way people in our church are dissatisfied with the church agreements we've had. Many of them think they want something different. They should be satisfied instead of wanting more of the pleasures of this world. Instead of looking to God and His Word for their guidance, they're busy looking at what other people are doing. They want new, exciting things."

Diane was quiet, thinking.

Grandpa continued, "That is why your mother and father don't let you do some things others do."

Diane looked at Maggie who was really uncomfortable reaching under that fence. She had a bare spot on her neck from like tries before where the board had rubbed all her fur off. Foolish Maggie. Diane didn't want to be like her.

"I didn't know," Diane said. "Maggie does help me understand it better."

"I know it's difficult to be different, especially when you're young, but try to obey your parents and trust them to know what's best."

"I'll try," Diane promised, meeting his gaze with a smile.

"Good girl," Grandpa approved. "Now I'd better get back into the house and finish my vacation since I have such good help. And I won't have to worry about those peas anymore since I know they're already eaten. That's a big worry off my mind."

"Grandpa!" Diane protested, but she was talking to his back as he slowly maneuvered his walker and headed for the house.

As she watched him go, Diane grinned happily. Grandpa truly was feeling better, and he had helped her feel differently about things her parents were asking her to do.

5
The Wounds of a Friend

"Don't say any more!" cried Laura.

"Maybe I should go," Margaret said gently. The eyes that looked at Laura were the eyes of Laura's old faithful friend.

"Yes, I believe you should," Laura answered with a waver in her voice.

When Margaret hugged Laura at the door, Laura briefly hugged back. She watched Margaret's slight frame as she got into her car, and when the dark head turned, she waved as always. Then the tears began to flow.

She hurried up to her room and dropped onto the bed, burying her wet cheeks in her pillow. Margaret! Her good friend from childhood had hurt her feelings dreadfully.

"You've become proud," Margaret had said.

Proud? Me? Laura asked herself. *I just want to look my best*, she argued, *and I'm just learning good taste.* But Margaret said

I'm getting proud.

It had all started because of Laura's job.

"It's a lot of fun," Laura had enthused to Margaret from the start. "Mrs. Linden is so nice. Her house is interesting and filled with beautiful stuff. You should see her teapot collection that I dusted today. Some of the teapots are fruit-shaped. One is a vine-covered cottage. Some are regular teapot shapes with flowers painted or molded on them. I wish you could see them."

"You are fortunate to have a good place to work," Margaret had said. "Our neighbors asked me to babysit at their place, but Mom and Dad said, 'Not at their house.' They didn't think the influence would be good. I was a little disappointed, but Mom needs me anyway. I have only brothers, except for Melinda, but she's only six."

"Maybe you'll get another chance," Laura comforted, and then she was off again on the benefits of her work. "They are Christian people; in fact, Mr. Linden is a preacher. Of course, they don't believe everything we believe. You should see their books. They have a whole room full of shelves loaded with books. Mrs. Linden said I could borrow any I wanted. Mom will have to okay them, but I'm sure there will be some good ones. Mr. Linden said he's glad to see a young person interested in reading because so many aren't anymore."

Margaret had listened and had told Laura she was happy for her. She wanted to be truly happy for Laura, but that night she lay in bed thinking over the conversation, jealousy rising within her. It simply didn't seem fair. Her offer wasn't a full-time job either, which would have been perfect. It would have given her time to help Mom.

Margaret turned the problem over to the Lord in prayer. She knew He helped her, because from that time on she could listen to Laura talk on and on without feeling any ill will.

Margaret listened to many tales of rich drapery and furniture. And Mr. and Mrs. Linden were so well-mannered. They looked for the good in everyone. Right away they spotted Laura's love of learning and encouraged her in it. They said she should go to college, but if she couldn't, she was smart enough to study on her own. She was a good worker, they said, and knew how to apply herself.

It wasn't long until Margaret began to have misgivings as she listened to Laura talk.

The Linden family had a party. One lady came early, and Laura was still there cleaning. Mr. Linden had introduced Laura as a "lovely young lady." Laura laughed when she told Margaret the story, but her cheeks turned pink.

Margaret lay awake that night wondering if she should warn Laura of the danger. She didn't want to make Laura angry. That wouldn't help. What could she do? Again she prayed.

Then came the time Laura was fussing with her blonde hair, trying to wave it just so. She was talking about her favorite subject. "They have lovely parties. Everything is mannerly, yet relaxed. Pretty flowers are always on the table and the food is prettily arranged."

"Do you go to parties there?" Margaret asked with surprise.

"Well . . ." Laura diddled with her hair brush. "She wanted me to come and help prepare for the party. She asked me to cut the flowers for the table and set it. And sometimes I help clean up the next day."

"But how do you know about manners and all that?" Margaret wondered.

"Well, I did go one time. She wanted me to meet some friends."

"Do your parents know?"

"No, they were busy getting ready to go away overnight that evening. They didn't ask and I didn't tell them."

"Who were the friends you were supposed to meet?"

Laura's face grew rosy. "I don't want to tell you." Both friends were quiet a few minutes. Then, "It was her grandson," Laura blurted. She looked directly at Margaret, as if to say, "Now, what do you think of that?"

Margaret breathed a quiet prayer. "Laura," she began, "I'm afraid this job isn't good for you."

"And why not? I'd like to know," Laura demanded boldly. "I enjoy it. I learn so much there, and they're Christian people."

Margaret hardly knew where to start, but she had to start somewhere. "They are flattering you too much. They are leading you into worldly ways."

"That won't happen. You don't need to worry."

"Laura, you are getting proud. Pride leads downhill."

It was then that Laura cried out, "Don't say any more!"

Now Laura sobbed into her pillow. Margaret had wounded her dreadfully. Margaret, her friend! How could a friend be so mean?

After a while the tears stopped coming and Laura lay thinking. She was beginning to see something she didn't want to see. *Margaret is so very, very right,* she thought. *The Lindens are flattering me, and I am starting to think I deserve more out of life than what I have because they tell me I am pretty and smart.*

"I was proud and now I am ashamed," she whispered to herself.

She sat up on the edge of her bed and looked unseeingly out of the window as she continued thinking. *I am glad Margaret told me. If I would have kept on being so dumb, where would I have ended up on that foolish road? Dear old Margaret. I'm glad I have a friend who told me the truth even when she knew I was going to get angry with her.*

She reached for her cell phone. "Sorry," she texted. "Thanks for being a true friend."

Faithful are the wounds of a friend.
Proverbs 27:6

6

We Want Risa

"We want Risa!" shouted Kelsey. "We want Risa!" She jumped up and down, making her ponytails bounce too.

"Esa, Esa," chanted her chubby two-year-old sister, Kate.

Sherry's heart fell. When her married sister, Tina, had said, "I'd like to have one of the girls help me tomorrow, Mom," her hopes had soared. Her nieces were sweet, and the work always seemed more fun than work at home.

Now the children wanted her other sister, Risa. That hurt. What was wrong with her?

Tina slipped her arm around Sherry's shoulders. She knew how Sherry felt.

"I think it's Sherry's turn," she told her daughters.

Sherry wanted to say, "That's okay. Let Risa go," but she was afraid she would cry if she said anything.

"Yes," said Mom, "it is her turn. I can drop her off at your place tomorrow. I have to go to town for parts for Dad anyway."

As soon as Tina and her children left, Sherry quietly told Mom, "I don't want to go. Can't Risa go instead?"

"But you love to go, and it's your turn," said Mom.

Sherry looked at the floor, her lips quivering. "The children don't want me."

"Oh, don't worry about what the children said today," Mom comforted. "Children change quickly. Tomorrow they'll be just as glad to see you as they would be to see Risa."

Sherry still didn't want to go where she wasn't wanted, but she couldn't see any way out. The next morning Mom dropped her off at Tina's house. As Mom had predicted, Kelsey came out on the sidewalk shouting excitedly, "Sherry's here! Sherry's here!"

Kate was trying to get her chubby little self down off the porch step so she could greet Sherry too.

Mom smiled a gentle "see what I mean" smile at Sherry.

Sherry smiled back and got out of the van. "See you later, Mom," she said as she shut the van door.

Sherry was still smiling as she took chattering Kelsey's hand and then scooped up Kate when they reached the porch. How could she help but smile? The children were so glad to see her. Her heart warmed, but still underneath she knew they preferred Risa. Sure, they liked her, but they liked Risa better. They had showed that yesterday, and it still hurt.

Well, she was here to help Tina. Taking the little girls with her, she found Tina in the kitchen. She was holding Baby Zach in one arm as she was putting milk in the fridge with the other hand.

"What do you want me to do?" Sherry asked.

"You can wash up the breakfast dishes. I've got to feed this hungry bear. I'll be back before long."

The dishes didn't take long. Sherry swept up the crumbs on the kitchen floor. The girls were playing nicely, so she went down to the basement to bring up some jars for the tomato juice they were going to can that day.

When Tina came back, she was surprised to see the work Sherry had done. "You're a fast worker," she said.

Sherry felt good inside. She knew it was true. Even if the children didn't like her as well as they liked Risa, she knew she was the faster worker of the two. But somehow she wasn't happy with being fast right now. She'd rather have the children like her as much as they liked Risa.

Together, Tina and Sherry worked at cutting up the tomatoes. When they had a panful scalded, Sherry hooked up the strainer outside the back door to juice them. The children came to watch.

"Be careful," Sherry warned. "They're hot!"

"—ot!" echoed Kate, and sat down on the grass to be out of the way.

Kelsey pouted, "I want to help. Mom lets me help."

"Well, I'm already done with these," said Sherry. "I need to take this juice into the house and get more tomatoes."

"You're mean," said Kelsey. "Risa would let us help."

Sherry stopped a second in her hurry to reach the house. She was mean? Why, she couldn't let them hurt themselves! She didn't want to be mean. She wanted to be liked!

Slowly she went on into the house.

Finding Tina, she said, "Kelsey wanted to help, but I told

her it was too hot. She said I was mean. Should I let her help?"

"No," said Tina. "She is short. The hot splashes would be right in her face, and she might pull the whole thing over trying to turn it. It wouldn't be safe."

"She told me Risa would let her," said Sherry. She could see Tina looking at her out of the corner of her eye, but she didn't look up.

"I think Risa would have said no too, but if she wouldn't have, I would have," replied Tina. "Kelsey is just too small for that job. Sherry, try not to worry too much about what Kelsey said yesterday. Children talk without thinking. God has made you and Risa different girls. You like to stick with the job at hand and then play if there's time. I can understand that. I like to do that too. Risa mixes play with work. That's okay, but sometimes I feel like telling her to get back to work when she stops to play with the children. Maybe she could work a little harder, and maybe we could both learn from her. Giving the children attention is important too. That's how they know we love them. I guess it takes a balance of both kinds of people in this world."

Sherry thought about Tina's words as she worked with the strainer and the tomatoes all morning. She tried to relax about the work enough to talk with Kelsey.

"Will you read to me when you're done?" asked Kelsey.

"Yes," promised Sherry, but Tina called for lunch just as the tomatoes were done.

"I'm sorry to interrupt you before you've cleaned up," Tina said. "Zach and Kate are getting tired and fussy. I need to feed them so they can get their naps."

After lunch, Tina said, "Bedtime, girls."

Sherry remembered her promise. She knew her mother would probably come for her before Kelsey got up from her nap. She looked at the cluttered table. She thought about the strainer outside with tomatoes skins drying on it. She made a decision.

"Is it all right if I read to Kelsey now?" she asked. "I'll clean up afterward."

"Sure, Sherry. I'm going to put Zach to bed and then take a nap myself since I have such good help today."

Kelsey snuggled close as Sherry held Kate. Together they read a book, and when Kelsey begged, they read another and then another. After a while Kate was sleeping, and Sherry put the girls in their beds.

Kelsey lay down contentedly. Sleepily she said, "I hope you come tomorrow, Sherry."

Sherry kissed her forehead. "I'd like that too," she said simply.

She went down the stairs with happiness circling her heart. It was easy to be liked after all. Tina was right. Children need love and sometimes the work can wait a little.

7
Words in Her Mouth

Karen barely heard the whir of the machines all around her. She was used to the sound. Her own sewing machine whirred and stopped, whirred and stopped, as she concentrated on her work. Her fingers placed a suit coat sleeve against the suit coat body, her knee pressed the sewing machine lever, and her machine sewed them together. All day long she sewed in coat sleeve after coat sleeve.

She arranged just so much fullness here and so much fullness there. There was no time to use pins. When she had been learning this job, she had ripped many stitches out because it was hard to get just the right amount of fullness at the top of the sleeve. She had sewn these sleeves in for months now, and it still frustrated her when her supervisor came over, held up a coat with her hand inside the sleeve, and declared that it didn't hang right. When that happened, Karen had to rip the sleeve out and do it over, thinking all the time about the units she wouldn't make that day (a certain number of sleeves made a unit). More units meant more money, but speed wasn't everything. The sewing had to be done just right.

Karen glanced up from her work at all the women sewing around her. Sewing machines were lined up along long tables. Each woman had her own particular seam to sew. Six women sewed sleeves like Karen did, while only two worked at some of the other jobs. This was because it took longer to sew in the sleeves just right. The sleeve sewers were not expected to sew as many coats per unit.

While Karen's fingers deftly sewed coat after coat, she had plenty of time to think. Her lips curved in an involuntary smile as the thought of her new joy. She had become a Christian at a young age, and for several years she had battled with confusion over what her conscience told her to do and what she saw other Christians doing. She had succumbed to some temptations in her confusion, but recently she had decided to go all the way with her Lord and follow her personal convictions in spite of what others did. She now faced life with renewed joy.

As she began taking time to study her Bible and pray for God's will in her life, she somehow felt this sewing factory wasn't the place for her. Surely she could find another job where she could do more for the Lord. Here the work sometimes seemed pointless and the atmosphere ungodly; however, she did have opportunities to witness. With this in mind, she tried to chat with the girls around her.

Her supervisor, Joan, often wanted to talk as she inspected Karen's work. Thought she was older and ungodly in her views, she seemed to appreciate Karen's Anabaptist lifestyle. Her being older made Karen unsure of how to talk with her.

Karen also talked with Pam, a girl her own age who sewed next to her. Already divorced at twenty, Pam's talk of boyfriends hinted at immorality. She was sure of herself in her ungodly lifestyle and held herself somewhat aloof from Karen.

Julie was also twenty and unmarried. Gentle, kind, and unassuming in her manner, she roomed with Pam, cheerfully doing most of the chores around their shared apartment. She would come over to Karen's machine during break to talk and ask questions. She sincerely wanted to know more about Karen's simple dress and lifestyle.

A few other Mennonite girls worked at this factory, but among hundreds of workers, they were only a handful. Karen hardly saw most of them, but she took her breaks with one girl near her and usually met with two from her church for lunch.

Once, Julie asked, "Why do you all wear something on your heads?"

"We wear it to show we are following Christ," explained Karen. "The Bible talks about this in 1 Corinthians 11. I can show you sometime if you'd like."

"I'll let you know," said Julie vaguely. "Got to go now. See you later."

Well, I offered, Karen thought. People can't be pushed. Sometimes they need time to think. And Julie did seem to be thinking.

One day just after lunch, Karen sat at her machine waiting for the work bell to ring. Julie came by and perched on the edge of the table to talk.

"The girls like you who work here all dress differently," she said with her typical abruptness. "Why is that?"

"We go to different churches," Karen said. "We all believe Christians should dress modestly and differently from the world, but the various churches have different rules about dress."

Julie nodded and got off the table when Karen's other neighbor, Maureen, came back to take her place at her machine. Maureen was an older, unhappy woman who was loud and nervous. She rarely noticed Julie. Today her quick movements seemed jerkier than ever, but she didn't say anything.

Julie asked another question. "But didn't you tell me one time that the girl you eat lunch with is from your church? She doesn't dress like you."

Karen wasn't sure how to answer at first. What Julie said was true, but Karen had never allowed the difference to bother her much. She answered with the only reason she could think of at the moment: "Her family came from another church, and she still does some things the way that church does."

Julie nodded and didn't say anything.

Angrily, Maureen jerked her thread through the machine and blurted, "God doesn't care if you wear a halter top to church."

Julie ignored Maureen and asked another question.

"Why *do* you dress the way you do, anyway?" she asked. Her voice emphasized the first "do."

Karen drew a deep breath. This was a big question. She'd already mentioned modesty. How could she go any deeper and still answer briefly?

Suddenly she clearly and calmly knew what she would say. Recently she had read something in her devotions that had made a lot of sense to her. Could she remember it right? It was in Numbers. God had explained to the children of Israel why He expected them to dress differently from those around them.

She began to answer slowly, trying to remember. "We dress the way we do for three reasons." Were there three? She tried hard to think how to word the reasons.

"First," she said aloud, surprised at how smoothly the words came out, "it reminds us who we are. Second, it protects us from sin. And third, it lets others know who we are."

Julie nodded her head. "That makes sense," she said.

The bell rang to get to work, and all discussion was over. Machines whirred busily, and so did Karen's mind. Just where had her answer come from? Sure, she had read the passage in Numbers and had pondered those verses, but she had never organized it into the three points she had told Julie. The words had just so simply fallen into place for her. God had helped her, she was sure. It was as if He'd put the words in her mouth.

"Thank you, God," she whispered. "Thank you for helping me know what to say."

Julie didn't come around to ask questions anymore, and Karen soon left the factory for another job. Years have passed, but she has never forgotten how God helped her, a young, inexperienced girl, answer a hard question in a short, clear manner.

Let the word of Christ dwell in you richly in all wisdom. Colossians 3:16.

Praying . . . that God would open unto us a door of utterance to speak the mystery of Christ. Colossians 4:3

8
One-of-a-Kind *Girl*

Seventeen-year-old Kay had never known a preacher's daughter who was her age until her family began attending Roaring Creek church. Kay watched the seventeen-year-old preacher's daughter to see if she was different in any way.

Carolyn looked nice enough. Her blonde hair curled in wisps about her face. She wasn't noticeably pretty, but she wasn't ugly either. She wasn't tall or short, fat or skinny. She turned and smiled warmly when she saw Kay looking at her. Kay turned away. She needed to make new friends here at Roaring Creek church, and she wasn't sure she wanted her first friend to be the preacher's daughter.

At the next youth meeting something happened that definitely put her with Carolyn, whether Kay wanted to be with her or not.

"Kay and Carolyn can be a pair," said the youth leader.

Kay looked at her cousin Aaron, who winked at her. He had attended Roaring Creek all his life, so she had asked him about Carolyn. He'd said she was just a regular girl.

Now he moved closer to Kay and whispered, "Give her a chance."

What choice did Kay have? They were supposed to help serve at the parents' supper, and the youth leaders told them to pour water.

Carolyn whispered, "You ask them if they want more water. I'll hold the pitcher and pour."

Hmm, she's shy, Kay thought. She had heard that ministers' daughters know everything and talk to anybody. Well, Kay didn't mind talking to people, so it would be easy enough to ask the parents if they wanted more water.

And then Kay found out Carolyn laughed easily. When they accidently dripped water on the floor, she laughed. When Kay had to ask Jeff's talkative father for the third time if he wanted more water, Carolyn laughed. By the time they were done, Carolyn had Kay laughing too.

"I like her," Kay confided to Aaron. "She's fun."

"I told you she's a regular girl," Aaron repeated.

Soon after the parents' supper, special meetings were held at the church, and Richard was the speaker. The Roaring Creek youth liked when Richard spoke. He was easy to listen to, and he set people on fire for the Lord. Several of the youth stood to recommit their lives to Christ. Carolyn went forward weeping. *What could she have done wrong?* Karen thought. *She's a minister's daughter, and they don't do anything wrong.*

Kay wanted to know, so she asked Carolyn about it.

"Oh," she said, "we're just as normal as anyone else. We can do wrong things too."

"Is it hard to be a minister's daughter?" Kay asked.

"Sometimes it seems people don't understand that we're just regular people, and they treat as differently. Sometimes I feel others are a little stiff and uncomfortable with me. Then I have to work extra hard to be friendly."

Kay blushed a little. She didn't know what to say.

After a pause, Carolyn continued, "I've heard that some people think we'd tattle to our dads about them. I'm not going to do that."

"That's ridiculous," Kay answered a little heatedly. "Our ministers aren't that picky. People shouldn't have anything to hide; then they wouldn't have to be afraid someone would tell on them."

"Well, I'm not hunting for stuff to tell my dad about. It's his job to lead the church, not mine. And then some think we're goody-goodies, but I don't think anyone can call me that. I don't feel any better than anyone else. Do you think I'm better than others?"

"At first I wasn't sure what to expect," Kay confessed, "but now that I know you, I like you. You're just a regular girl like Aaron said you are."

"Thanks!"

"It's just not fair," Kay sputtered angrily to Aaron later. "She's just a regular girl, and she can't help it that she's a minister's daughter. She needs friends just like anyone else."

"That's what I think," Aaron agreed. "People don't understand."

"But why can't they understand?" Kay questioned. "After all, it takes only a little common sense to see that."

"And a cousin named Aaron," he teased, looking to see what she would say.

"Well, yes, that too," Kay admitted, wrinkling her nose at him. "But it's mainly that I'm learning to know her."

"You gave her a chance to be your friend."

"She's not just an ordinary friend," Kay said. "She's friendlier and more thoughtful than my other friends. She's a friend who's one of a kind."

"Wait a minute," Aaron interrupted. "Do I understand what you're saying? You said Carolyn is a regular girl, but now you're saying she's one of a kind. How can that be?"

Kay was caught with her mouth open. She had been ready to praise her friend more, but instead she closed her mouth. Aaron was right. What did she think about Carolyn anyway?

Aaron was laughing, but Kay insisted heatedly, "Every word I said is true. She's a regular girl, and she's a special friend too."

"Now that makes more sense," he said. "You've enjoyed her friendship as a regular girl and now she's your special friend."

"Exactly," Kay agreed, "but it is more than that. I think she's a better friend because she has to work harder to make friends."

"So is it a good thing that people think she's odd because she's a minister's daughter?"

"Not really," Kay answered. "It's just that Carolyn has turned a potentially awkward role into good by doing her best."

Aaron was still looking at Kay thoughtfully. "Is it possible?"

he began, then stopped and started again. "Is it possible that ministers' girls can be any kind of girl just like other girls can? You've got talkative girls, quiet girls, busy girls, and lazy girls." He pretended to count them on his fingers. "There are thoughtful girls, rude girls—really, just all kinds of girls. Don't you think a minister's daughter can be any of those too?"

"I suppose so," Kay admitted. "Minister's daughters are just regular girls, but they walk a different path than the rest of us do."

"That's it," he said. "They are regular girls in a different situation. But then, we all have different situations, so I still vote to just call them regular girls."

And Kay couldn't say anything against that.

9

Parakeet Friend

Doris hurried to the school van as soon as the closing song was sung.

"Hi," she responded gloomily to Marlene's mom's "Hello" as she climbed in.

Soon Marlene got in and sat beside her as she always did. "What are you going to do tonight?" she asked.

Doris shrugged and looked out the window at the trees.

"What's wrong?" Marlene asked.

Doris shrugged again and continued looking out the window. If Marlene didn't know what was wrong, she wasn't going to tell her. How could a best friend like Marlene treat her as she had treated her today? Why, Marlene and she had been best friends for years. They had always traveled to school together because they lived close to each other. Even though there were other girls in their classroom, they were the only two eighth graders. They had always shared everything. That was what was so hard about what Marlene had done. That new girl, Edna, was going to be a problem. Marlene didn't need to forget her old friends and be so friendly to Edna.

As soon as Doris got home, she asked her sister Donna, "Where's Mom?"

"She went over to Grandma to help her with something. She'll be home soon."

Doris moped around the house awhile and then decided to get her school work out. When she walked through the kitchen, her parakeet Sunny chirped at her.

"Sure, Sunny," she said. "You can be out for a while."

She opened the door of his cage and put her hand in. Sunny hopped onto her outstretched index finger and hung on as she withdrew her hand.

Sitting down at the table, she got her school books out. Sunny hopped around on her books and started pecking her social studies paper when she got it out.

"No!" she exclaimed, putting her hand over the page. She gave him scratch paper, which he nibbled contentedly while she finished social studies.

"Now, Sunny, I need that paper," she said. "I need it to do my math." When she took the paper from him, he flew to the window and sat on the curtain rod. He sat there chittering to the sparrows outside the window while she finished her schoolwork.

"Now you have to go back in your cage," she said, walking over to the window and holding out her finger again. He hopped on for the ride back to his cage.

"Sunny," she said after he was back in the cage, "thanks for being my friend. I need a good friend about now."

That evening Uncle Paul stopped in to visit. Then it was bedtime, and it wasn't until after Doris had gone to her room that she remembered about Marlene and the new girl. It was too late to talk to Mom now. Oh well, maybe tomorrow would go better. She'd give Marlene another chance.

The next morning Doris climbed into the van with a bright smile and a cheery "Good morning!" for Marlene. Marlene was the same as ever, and they chatted merrily the whole way to school. The day was off to a good start.

At first recess Doris lingered inside for a few minutes before heading out the door. Then she saw them: Marlene and Edna were talking again. And worse, they started walking away as she got near to them. Doris hesitated and then walked to the nearby merry-go-round. *I don't want to look like I'm chasing after them,* she thought.

Soon she got up and wandered into the schoolhouse. Maybe she could help Teacher Anne, who was working on her bulletin board. "May I help with that?" she asked.

"Sure," answered Teacher Anne. "You can hand me these letters as I put them up."

As Doris handed up the red paper letters, she said, "Marlene doesn't want to be my friend anymore."

"Oh, are you sure?" asked Teacher Anne.

"Yes, she and that new girl, Edna, just walked away when I got close."

"That doesn't seem like Marlene. Are you sure they saw you?"

"I don't know how they could help but see me," insisted Doris. "I was right there."

"I'm glad that Marlene is being a friend to the new girl," commented Teacher Anne.

"Yes, I know," admitted Doris. "It's just that she should let me be a friend too."

"I'll try to watch what's going on," promised Teacher Anne. "I still don't think Marlene would purposefully exclude you."

"Teacher Anne didn't believe me," Doris complained to her mother that evening. "It was true too. They just walked away from me."

"Marlene is a kind girl," Mom said. "She wouldn't be rude intentionally. And it's good she's kind to the new girl."

Doris felt tears well behind her eyes. No one believed her.

Suddenly Sunny jumped onto the side of his cage, setting it swinging as he scolded loudly.

Mom laughed. "He wants to be in on this too."

Doris smiled a little. Sunny was funny.

"Do you remember when we first brought Sunny home?" asked Mom. "Remember how he scolded and bit us when we tried to hold him at first?"

"Yes," answered Doris. "We tried to hold him in our hands like we did Michel's hamster. He didn't like that. He just wanted to sit on my finger."

"I think maybe your friendship with Marlene is a bit like that. Maybe you are holding on too tightly. Maybe you need to release her some. You two have been the only girls in the same grade at school for a long time. You live close to each other. You are very close friends, but it's good to have other friends too."

Doris turned away. Mom didn't understand either.

She turned to Sunny. "You like me, anyway," she whispered. Sunny's seed dish was full of empty shells. She snapped it out to refill it. She got him fresh water too. Then she got him out on her finger and brought him close to her face. Sunny scooted closer on her finger and reached out to rub his beak on her nose in a parakeet kiss.

Doris chuckled and felt a lot better. Sunny was such a funny friend. She thought about how he had hated to be held in a curled up fist but liked to sit on her finger. He didn't fly away unless he was startled. He wanted to be held, but he didn't like to be held tightly.

Was her friendship with Marlene like that, as Mom had said? Maybe she was being selfish.

"I'll share her with the new girl," she whispered to Sunny. "I'll not hold Marlene too close. I'll let her be friends with that new girl, but I hope she still will like me too. I hope all three of us can be friends together."

10
A Monster in the House

Noisy chatter filled the Larky house as Traci and Rena washed the breakfast dishes, glad for a Saturday at home. Traci scrubbed the dishes in the warm sudsy water and rinsed them while Rena lifted them, dripping, from the rack to dry them.

In the next room, Grandma heard their voices becoming louder and louder. She paused from her mending and looked toward the kitchen.

"Mom just likes you better than me," came an angry voice through the doorway.

Grandma laid aside her sewing and started to get up. Then she changed her mind. She stayed seated and listened carefully for a few minutes. She didn't hear any more words, but the dishes clattered extra noisily. She sighed and picked up her work. She had never noticed her daughter, the girls' mother, showing any favoritism. What was wrong? Her mind traveled back to her own childhood and youth struggles.

One evening the next week, Grandma offered to dry the dishes for Traci. Traci, of course, was glad to work with Grandma. "So, do you think your mom likes Rena better than you?" Grandma began as she dried the dishes.

"Yes, it's true," Traci said. "Mom scolds me all the time but she never scolds Rena. Rena's the good little girl."

Grandma paused with her dish towel in her hand, waiting for the next dish. She looked directly at Traci. "What kind of things does she scold you for?"

"Oh, I don't know." Traci's cloth went slowly around and around a mixing bowl in the dish water. "It's always, stop this and stop that. It's whatever. She's always scolding me. As soon as Rena complains, Mom scolds me. When I complain about Rena, Mom hardly says anything."

"Yes, I know exactly how you feel," said Grandma.

Traci stopped drying dishes and looked at Grandma wonderingly. Grandma was agreeing with her?

Grandma smiled back. Then she asked, "Is there anyone else who sees this like you do?"

"Do you know Shyla?" Traci asked, looking at Grandma eagerly. "She's that new lady at church who has the cute curly-headed baby. I babysit for her sometimes. She believes me when I talk to her."

"I see," said Grandma slowly. "May I talk to her about this problem?"

"No." Traci looked angry again. She shook her head for added emphasis.

"I think I do need to talk to your mom though," suggested Grandma.

"No, please don't," Traci insisted.

"But I think she'd like to know how you feel," pleaded Grandma. "I'm sure she's not trying to do this."

"No, don't!" Traci vigorously scrubbed dishes and was silent.

Grandma carefully watched her granddaughters and their mother carefully. It seemed to her the girls' mother was fair with both girls. They both had chores to do. They both had to finish homework. She asked both how school had gone. Actually, Grandma thought the girls' mother talked more to Traci, probably because Traci had more to say.

Meanwhile, Traci's mind was racing. *Grandma said she knows how I feel. What did she mean anyway?*

One day Mom and Rena were working in the garden. Grandma was sewing, and Traci was washing the breakfast dishes alone. When she finished the dishes, she paused in the doorway. Dare she ask Grandma what she'd meant?

"Grandma," she began quickly before her bravery left, "you said you understand that I feel Mom likes Rena better than me. What did you mean?"

"I do understand," answered Grandma. "I was there once myself. I was the oldest in my family. I had one little sister after a row of brothers. My little sister was Mama's girl. She was quiet and never caused any trouble. She never said things that upset Mom like I did. I felt I was always in trouble.

"My parents seemed so strict; they said no to nearly everything I wanted to do, but when my little sister came along eight years after me, my parents relaxed their rules a little. I was angry about this and felt my mother didn't love me."

"Really?" asked Traci incredulously. "What did you do?"

"Nothing," answered Grandma. "I didn't do anything until I grew up."

"What did you do then?"

"I began to understand that some of it was my fault," said Grandma, smiling kindly at Traci. "I was a girl who had my own ideas about everything. I didn't like to listen. I was always talking about my own ideas. It's no wonder my mother would prefer to be with my quiet sister, but I really believe now that my mother loved me the same and tried to be fair. It's just that I needed a lot more supervision and correction. I got into trouble more and it was difficult for me to understand that. I struggled for years before I learned to be thankful for my parents' seeming strictness."

She paused and Traci said, "I'm not like that."

"No," said Grandma, "we're all different. The most important thing I learned in this whole thing was that the devil wanted me to be jealous. He even used a friend to sympathize with me and make me feel more unloved and jealous of my sister. This friend would believe every word I said, and together we made it a worse case than what it was. Jealousy is a sin and something we all struggle with. The Bible says jealousy is as cruel as the grave. It can ruin our lives because it makes us very unhappy."

Traci was quiet. She stood in the doorway looking at Grandma.

"Come here," said Grandma. When Traci stood beside her, Grandma put her hand on her arm. "I do understand, and it's hard."

Traci's eyes became little pools of tears. She swallowed. "You don't think I'm just trying to be jealous, do you? Am I just to ignore it when Mom isn't fair?"

"No, honey," said Grandma. "I know you're not trying to be jealous. But you must believe your mom does love you. She is trying to be fair with both of you girls. Don't listen to Satan when he tells you she doesn't love you. Pray instead of keeping on thinking about it. Ask God to help you have a good relationship with your mother. We could pray together now. Would you like that?"

Traci nodded wordlessly.

Together the gray head and the brown head bowed before the One who knew all about them. Grandma asked Him to help Traci understand her feelings and not hold anything against her mother. Traci prayed too.

It wasn't easy, but Traci gradually began to see jealousy as the ugly monster it was. Every time she felt angry and jealous, she told herself, *Jealousy is a sin. I can't let myself be jealous.* She prayed to be delivered from evil thoughts. At Grandma's advice, she refused to talk about it to anyone other than Grandma and Mom, not even to Shyla. As Grandma had said, it wasn't fair to talk about Mom to others when Mom herself knew nothing about it.

Jealousy is as cruel as the grave.
Song of Solomon 8:6

11
A Little Tongue

Something was wrong. Janna could feel it. Conversations between her and Michelle were awkward. Would their friendship ever get back to what it had been? She felt terrible about losing Michelle's close friendship, but what could she do about it?

When Janna had first noticed Michelle's coolness, she had asked what was wrong.

"Nothing," was Michelle's answer, but when her eyes refused to meet Janna's, Janna knew something was wrong.

After asking for the third time, "What's wrong? What I have I done?" Janna got her first clue what the problem was.

"You should know," Michelle muttered.

"But I don't know," Janna protested.

Michelle was quiet for a minute. Then in a low but accusing tone she said, "I told you some of Tim's struggles. I needed to talk to somebody because I was so worried about my big brother's Christian life. I told you not to tell anybody, but you did!"

"I didn't tell anybody."

"Yes, you did!" Michelle insisted, looking at Janna now. "You know you did."

"I . . ." Janna began, but her voice trailed off. She was remembering. Mona had said Tim hadn't been himself. Janna had answered that she was worried too. And then some things had slipped out of Janna's mouth. She realized she had been telling too much, so she had told Mona not to tell. Mona had promised not to tell just like Janna had promised Michelle.

Mona, Janna now thought angrily, *why did you do this to me? I told you not to tell.* But this thought was quickly followed by another. *Who says Mona had told?*

"Why are you so sure I told someone?" Janna asked Michelle quietly.

"You're my closest friend. You are the only one besides my parents I talked to. Who else would have told?"

"But . . ." Janna paused, searching for a way out of admitting her fault. "What did you hear that I said?"

"You don't want to admit the truth, do you?" asked Michelle in her usual blunt way. "Lily told me she was praying for Tim. I said, 'What do you mean?' She said. 'Tina told me he's having some struggles.' She said he's thinking about giving up the Christian faith."

"I never said that," Janna retorted angrily.

"Well," answered Michelle, "I told her that was far from the truth, and I asked her where she heard that. She said Mona told her, and she knew it was true because Mona told her she heard it straight from my best friend."

Mona, Janna groaned inwardly, *you really goofed.*

"I told only Mona," Janna said. "Mona said she was concerned about Tim because he hadn't been himself. She seemed really concerned about him. I was too, after I had talked to you. He'd been on my mind a lot and I'd been praying for him. I told her a few things without thinking. When I remembered that I had promised you not to talk to anyone, I stopped and told her not to tell anyone. She promised me she wouldn't, but she lied to me."

Did she do anything you didn't do? the Spirit said to Janna. *Maybe Mona accidentally told only one person too. It takes only one at a time for many to hear about it.*

Janna couldn't look Michelle in the eye. She studied the blue flowers on her dress skirt. There was no way out. She had been wrong. Janna lifted her head and looked straight at Michelle. "I'm sorry. I was wrong. I should have been more careful to not say one word. After all, I did promise."

"It's okay," Michelle whispered as she wiped her eyes with her hands.

Janna wiped a few tears too. "We only wanted to help. Mona was concerned too."

"I know," Michelle whispered. Another tear rolled down her cheek when she looked at Janna. "I know you both have kind hearts and only want to help, but when people start saying things are worse than they really are, it will hurt and discourage Tim if he hears it—and he probably will hear about it. Someone who is concerned about Tim will hear about it and try to talk to him."

What Michelle said was true. Janna sure wished she'd kept her mouth shut. She could have talked to Mona about Tim without telling her what Michelle had said. Janna had to admit in her heart that she had enjoyed telling Mona something new, and her motive hadn't been love. She could have asked what they could do to encourage him.

Time went on. Tim heard the false reports going around about him, and he was angry. Though Janna didn't think it was all her fault, she knew she'd had a hand in it. The worst thing was that she couldn't undo it. After praying about it and asking Michelle what she could do, she knew the only thing she could do was to go to Tim and beg his forgiveness.

Janna gathered up her courage and approached Tim. She tried to explain that she'd had an innocent hand in one of the false rumors, but was very, very sorry. He only looked at Janna silently with blazing blue eyes and mumbled something before he walked away.

Janna didn't know if her apology would do any good, but she had done what she could. Now she could only pray that God would use it to help Tim forgive her and all the others who had helped spread untruth about him. Janna prayed that Tim would see that the church people really did love him despite their humanness.

Janna also prayed for Michelle. She knew Michelle was trying her hardest to forgive her, but the old closeness between them was gone. Although Janna regretted it with all her heart, she knew it would take a long time to mend the friendship. Would Michelle ever be able to trust her fully again? Only God knew. And only God knew what direction Tim would take in life.

> Even so the tongue is a little member, and boasteth great things. Behold, how great a matter a little fire kindleth! James 3:5

12

Give Some, Save Some, Spend Some

It was the perfect summer job. Working part-time for Aunt Sue at the market was fun. It gave Joan time to be with her cousin Lettie, and she earned more money than she ever did before.

She and Lettie talked about that money.

"I can buy new dresses and new shoes," said Lettie.

"It's going to be so fun to buy food at the market," said Joan. "It will be my money and my choice."

"I know," said Lettie. "I never before had so much money of my own."

The first day at market was a cool spring morning. Joan's jacket felt good. The two girls helped Aunt Sue set out jars of pickles and jellies for sale. Lettie arranged a basket of homemade soaps while Joan put lettuce and spring onions in neat rows.

Aunt Sue talked to the market manager while the girls

finished. "It's nice to have help," she told him. "Last year I had a friend come to help me, but she couldn't come every day. That wasn't a problem in the spring, but in the summer when more things grew in my garden, I wished for full-time help. Soon we'll be getting busier as the strawberries ripen, so I'll have plenty of work for two girls. With both of them hired for the whole summer, I should always have the help I need."

Before long, Aunt Sue sold their first customer some jelly and some spring lettuce.

"Here, girls," she said after the customer left. "Let me show you where I keep my money and tell you how to give change."

After their lesson she asked, "What are you girls going to do with the money you earn?"

Lettie shrugged. "Lots of things."

Joan added, "I'm not sure. There are lots of things I could do with it. It's going to be fun to have money of my own."

Aunt Sue chuckled. The space between her front teeth showed when she smiled, but her eyes sparkled in her pleasant face. "I'm glad I can help you earn some money," she said. "A first payday is exciting. I'll give you some advice my dad gave me when I started to earn money. He said, 'Give some, save some, and then spend some.' "

"Hello there," she greeted another customer. "How was your winter?"

The thin, elderly man told Aunt Sue about his health problems while she listened sympathetically. "But praise the Lord, warm weather always comes and then my bones don't ache as much," he finished. Then pointing his cane at the two girls, he asked, "Who do we have here?"

"These are my nieces," said Aunt Sue. "They're going to work for me this summer."

"Well, pay them well and make them work for it. They need to learn the value of a dollar when they're young."

"I'll try," answered Aunt Sue as she slipped a jar of strawberry jam into a bag. "Hope to see you every week."

"Oh, you will," he said. Before he left, he pointed his cane at the girls again. "Don't you girls go wasting your money either," he ordered.

"We won't," answered Joan, the braver of the two.

Aunt Sue watched the old man as he walked slowly away. "That is the best part of this job," she told the girls. "I enjoy meeting people. It's a wonderful opportunity to share with them about the Lord too.

"Back to money and my dad's advice. 'Give some,' is giving some to the Lord. We can give through the church or some other trusted organization. Helping someone else with part of your money is commanded in the Bible. God blesses those who give. Next, it's important to save for a rainy day, as the old saying goes.

"Now here are two customers. One for me and one for you, Joan. Lettie can have the next one. Just say hi and smile. Ask them if you can help them."

Later Aunt Sue continued her advice. "I'll feel bad if you girls spend all your money. You should have a sizable chunk when this summer is over. There are fifteen market days, and I'm giving each of you $20 a day. That adds up to $300."

"Wow!" exclaimed Lettie. "Maybe I can buy some furniture for my room."

"Well, if you look for a used piece, you certainly could," replied Aunt Sue. "But you would have to save at least half of your money. You should give at least a tenth, which is $2 each week. That leaves you with $18. If you saved half of that each week for fifteen weeks, you'd have $135. That would buy a piece of used furniture."

"If I work hard and earn money," said Joan slowly, "I think I'd like to spend a little just for fun too."

"I think that's okay," said Aunt Sue. "The best way to do that is to separate a small amount each week for things like that and never spend more than you put aside. You call that budgeting. You plan ahead. You think, *After I tithe, I need to save some and pay for this and spend for that.* That way you know exactly how much you have to spend."

Lettie was excited about the advice. She began doing some figuring on a piece of paper, whispering to herself. Joan watched with amusement. She didn't think she needed to be so careful.

She began planning in her head. She could do a lot with that much money. She'd never before gotten money every week. It was going to be fun to have spending money in her pocket all the time.

The summer passed swiftly for Joan. She enjoyed the job as much as she thought she would, but the most fun thing was having money of her own to spend.

She followed Aunt Sue's advice about giving some. She skipped a few times, but most Sundays some of her pay went into the offering basket.

Hot summer days at the market called for cold drinks.

Mom said Joan should take her own drink from home and save her money for bigger things, but Joan thought she would have money for both. Sometimes the cold drink seemed to call for a candy bar or something else to go with it. Joan had money for that too.

The last day of market came and the girls were back in school. One day Lettie invited Joan and some other friends to her house for a Sunday afternoon.

She took them to her room to show them a new matching bedspread and curtains. Joan looked at the blue and yellow quilt and the gingham yellow curtains. They were beautiful.

"You bought them yourself?" asked Julie. "Where did you get that much money?"

"Joan and I worked for Aunt Sue at the market this summer," explained Lettie.

"What did you buy, Joan?" The girls turned to Joan with listening ears.

Joan shrugged. "I'm still deciding."

The girls chattered on about favorite colors for rooms, but Joan wasn't listening.

She had been planning to buy two new dresses. That was all the money she had left. She didn't have enough to make any big purchases. Drinks, snacks, and cheap, pretty things she didn't need had used up most of her money.

She sat on the bed with the other girls as they jumped from one subject to the next. She was quiet, thinking. She softly touched the blue flowered fabric in the quilt. It was beautiful. How she wished she hadn't wasted her money.

13
Only a Thistle

Leann was glad for a summer job. She needed the money. At first she was afraid she couldn't weed Mrs. Rhodes' flower beds without making a mistake. Prior to beginning her job, she had weeded her married sister's flowers and pulled out a perennial plant planted just the year before. Her sister had been cross about that.

"Don't worry about pulling out the wrong plants in my gardens," Mrs. Rhodes said. "My perennials are well established. You'll be able to recognize them by their size. Even if you do pull one out, there are plenty more."

Leanne found that this weeding wasn't that hard. She recognized the weeds growing in Mrs. Rhodes' garden as the same ones growing in her mother's vegetable garden. And the perennial plants were easy to see after she had pulled the weeds.

But Leann had one other worry: Mr. Rhodes. He had come out on her first day of work and stood there silent and sober while Mrs. Rhodes had explained the work.

"I don't know why this is necessary," he had complained to Mrs. Rhodes. "I can still mow, you know. We could put all of this into grass."

Mrs. Rhodes had calmly patted his arm. "But think how much we enjoy the flowers, and the birds and butterflies they bring. Let's give it a try."

He hadn't answered. As it turned out, Leann didn't have to worry about him either. He left it to Mrs. Rhodes to supervise Leann's work.

As Leann weeded, she thought of how much money she would make in one week and then in a couple of weeks. She knew what she wanted to do with her money. The girls at her church had been wearing trendy nightwear at their sleepovers, and she hoped she could persuade her mother to let her buy some too before the next sleepover. Mother had she said she didn't think the latest styles were appropriate to wear even at bedtime, but surely if Leann used her own money . . .

Working in the garden was fun. The Rhodes lived in town and had a large backyard enclosed by a high white picket fence. The flower beds were sprawled along the inside of the fence. At one corner the flower beds spread out around a birdbath and a garden shed that looked just like a playhouse with its shuttered windows and front porch. Birds and butterflies enjoyed the garden too. Bird songs and the sweet smell of flowers made it a very pleasant place to work.

Once in a while Mrs. Rhodes came out to ask her to move a crowded plant to a new location, but most of the time Leann worked alone. One day as she was working, something pricked her hand.

"Ouch!" She hadn't seen the small thistle.

I'll let it go for now, she decided. *It's hard to see. Next week I'll bring gloves to pull it out.* But the next week she forgot her gloves, and by the following week she forgot the thistle altogether. When she got to work the third week, Mr. Rhodes was waiting for her.

"Come with me," he ordered. His bushy eyebrows were pulled down and his jaw set. "Look at that," he said, pointing his long stern finger at the thistle she'd skipped. It was much taller than the plants around it and even sported a couple of purple blooms. "That," he said, "is a *Cirsium vulgare,* commonly known as a thistle. We don't grow them in our garden. I want you to pull it out."

Leann swallowed nervously. That thing was even pricklier now. How could she pull it out without her gloves? Mr. Rhodes was watching her.

"Go to the garden shed," he said as though reading her thoughts. "A spade is hanging just inside the door on the right. Get it, and dig this thing out now."

Leann did as he said. They both stood looking at the tall thistle now lying in the yard.

"Take it out to the garbage can on the other side of the fence," Mr. Rhodes commanded. "And don't you let one of those things grow again." His tall, thin figure stalked stiffly back into the house.

How had that thistle grown so fast? Leann wiped away a tear with the back of her hand. She was glad Mrs. Rhodes hadn't come out with her husband. Her embarrassment faded after a while, but Leann knew she would never let this happen again. After all, a thistle, when it is small, isn't hard to pull out.

If Mrs. Rhodes knew anything about it, she never said anything. She kept saying she was happy with Leann's work.

At bedtime a few days later, Leann read the parable of the sower in the fourth chapter of Mark. The sower sowed his seed by throwing it out by handfuls. Some of the seeds fell in places too hard for them to grow, and the birds ate them. Other seeds fell among rocks. These sprouted but soon died because there wasn't enough soil.

Then she read the next verse. "These are they which are sown among thorns; such as hear the word, and the cares of this world and the deceitfulness of riches, and the lusts of other things entering in choke the word, and it becometh unfruitful."

In her mind she again saw the ungainly thistle towering over the flowers in Mrs. Rhodes flowerbed. It had grown so fast! If that thistle had been allowed to grow and go to seed, more thistles would have grown. Eventually they would have choked out the flowers.

She thought about how excited she was to buy that stylish nightwear for the sleepover. Was that an example of the lusts of other things referred to in this parable?

God spoke directly to her heart. *Yes, love for those clothes is a thistle in your life. Pull it out.*

I will, she promised silently. *Oh, I will. I don't want any lusts to take over my heart.*

She rested her hand lightly on the open page of her Bible and looked up, her mind deep in thought. She'd wear the clothes her mother had chosen for her and let her friends think what they wanted. If they thought she was old-fashioned, it didn't matter. She was going to do what was right for her.

14

Strict Mom

"*Mom, for our spring program* at school this year, the girls are going to wear different colors of the same fabric," Bonnie said excitedly. "Benny's store has it and Lakin's store has it too. They have it in dark blue, maroon, and purple. I saw the blue and it is gorgeous. It's dark, but not too dark, and has black vines all over. Each girl is going to get the color she wants."

"That sounds nice," answered Mom. "We'll have to go to one of those stores soon, but not this week anymore. I have to help Dad with some bookwork this week."

Bonnie frowned. "We can't wait, Mom. They might already be sold out." She didn't like to wait for anything, especially not for a trip to a fabric store now that she was learning to sew. The new fabric smell and the many colors and designs to choose from were so exciting.

"Oh, Bonnie, you worry too much. If both stores have

the fabric, there'll be plenty. And I'm sure we could get it at other stores farther from home too." Mom wouldn't budge, so Bonnie waited impatiently for next week.

On Monday morning before leaving for school, Bonnie asked, "Mom, will we go to the fabric store today?"

"Today I need to wash," replied Mom. "Tomorrow will suit me a lot better."

That day at school the girls talked excitedly about the beautiful fabric, though many of them had not seen it yet. On Tuesday Bonnie thought about that dress material all day. Lucille said she was going to pick maroon, and Bonnie thought she would like that color best too.

Finally the school day was over and Bonnie raced to the van. Mom was taking them to the fabric store that very afternoon! It wasn't unusual for the family to visit fabric stores; after all, Mom sewed dresses for herself and her four daughters. But today was special! Bonnie would pick out her program dress.

Not everyone in the family was excited about shopping for fabric, though. Bonnie's brother complained vehemently, "Shopping is so boring! You have enough dresses anyway."

"You can stay in the van and do your homework if you don't want to go into the store," Mom suggested. Bonnie's brother still grumbled, but decided staying on the van was better than going into a fabric store.

Bonnie's excitement grew as she entered the store. Usually she looked at all the fabrics and thought about projects she could do, but today her mind was on one certain fabric.

There it was! Bonnie's fingers went out to touch the beautiful fabric. It had a nice soft feel and wasn't too slippery. All the colors were gorgeous, but she liked the maroon best of all.

"This one," she said to Mom.

Mom looked silently at the fabric for several seconds. Then, "It's more red than maroon, Bonnie. I'm afraid it's too bright."

"But Mom," pleaded Bonnie, "Lucille is getting it. I want to have the same color she has. It will be all right."

"Hmm, let's get it out of the row so we can see it better," Mom said.

Oh no, this isn't sounding good. Aloud, Bonnie said, "Other girls will be wearing it. It's okay."

"Let me unfold some of it and hold it up," Mom said. "I'll get the purple out too and hold it beside this one. You back up a little and look at them."

Bonnie looked. She had to admit that the maroon was brighter, but would it matter? Other girls would get it, she was sure.

To her mother she said, "Lucille is getting it, and her mom's picky about colors too. I know it will be all right."

"Are you sure she's getting it?" asked Mom. "Did her mom buy it?"

"Well, not yet," Bonnie admitted. "But she will, because it's what Lucille wants."

"No," said Mom in her final voice. "That shade of red will really stand out against the purple and blue dresses, and the black pants the boys are wearing. Dad and I don't want our daughter to stand out like that. You have to choose one of the other colors."

Bonnie's face fell, but she knew it was no use to argue. She chose the blue. It was pretty too, but as they drove home, she was as sad as she'd been happy on the way to the store. She just knew others would get that maroon fabric. Why did she have to have such a strict mom who wouldn't let her be like her friends? It wasn't fair.

Bonnie tried to find out what the other girls had bought, but somehow she was never at the right place at the right time to hear. And she was afraid to ask. What if she was the only one with blue? She would look like an oddball. Why did her mom always want her to be an oddball?

The program date wasn't far away. For two weeks the students practiced their songs. The last week they practiced almost every day. Bonnie enjoyed program practice, but this year, when she thought of that maroon fabric, she didn't enjoy it quite as much.

Mom sewed the blue dress, and Bonnie had to admit she liked it. It fit well and the color was nice, but why couldn't she have that maroon material? She was sure other girls would have it. And she had so wanted to be like Lucille.

The day of the program came. The school practiced all morning at the building where the program would be given. After school, all was bustle at Bonnie's house as they got ready.

"Where are my black pants?" her brother asked with a worried look.

"Oh, here they are," said Mom. "I pressed them for you and forgot to put them back."

It was no wonder she had forgotten. She had made dresses for two of Bonnie's little sisters too. Bonnie knew Mom had worked hard to get all that sewing done in addition to her usual work. But Bonnie also knew Mom didn't mind. She loved to do things for her children.

Except to get me the fabric I wanted, Bonnie thought

grumpily. *My mom is so strict. I think we have the strictest mom at church. She fusses more about clothes than anyone else.*

Bonnie had butterflies in her stomach on the way to the evening program. She always did when she knew she would have to sing in front of a crowd of people. But this year she had a second worry—her dress. It was the first year the students had picked different colors, and she didn't want to be the only one in blue. What if all the others wore purple and maroon? She would be a terrific oddball then.

As Bonnie walked toward the building, she looked around for some of the other high school girls. Seeing no one, she entered and slowly hung up her coat. Soon she was going to find out which colors the other girls had chosen.

Then she saw Doreen and Vivian. They wore purple. Rhonda and Lucille soon showed up. They both wore blue! Relief washed over Bonnie. Wearing a big smile, she greeted her friends. She soon spotted the remaining two girls. One wore purple and one wore blue. There was no maroon!

The program went without a hitch. Afterward, Bonnie listened to the chatter.

"Mom said the maroon fabric was too red," said one.

"Yeah, my mom said it was too bright," another said.

Oh my! Bonnie gasped. *I guess my mom isn't the only mom after all who thought that fabric was too bright.*

After that night, whenever Mom and Bonnie disagreed about clothes, Bonnie remembered the program dress. Mom had been right about that dress, and Bonnie would always think, *Probably she's right this time too. Moms just know more about some things.*

15
Plenty of Time

Gina smelled coffee. She heard birds twittering in the tree branches just outside her bedroom window. Rolling over, she stretched luxuriously. It was a wonderful feeling to wake up and not have to hurry to get ready for school. It was June, and summer vacation had started a week ago.

"Gina, time to get up," Mom's voice called up the stairs.

Gina sighed but got up right away. What a glorious day stretched ahead of her! Mom was sure to have work for her, but Uncle Dan's family was coming in time for supper that evening. It would be so special to see Cousin Eva again. She and her family lived out of state and didn't visit often.

"Mom, what time did you say Uncle Dan and his family are coming?" Gina asked as she reached the bottom step.

"They weren't sure," answered Mom, looking up from a frying pan full of pancakes. "I told them we'd plan to eat at five, but they thought they'd arrive before that."

"I hope they do. I'm ready to see Eva again."

As soon as the family settled around the table and the blessing was asked, Mom began talking about Gina's little sister Julie. She had been a preemie and still sometimes needed special care. Though four now, she caught pneumonia easily and had been hospitalized once. Last night she had coughed a lot and still ran a fever this morning.

"I think she'd better go to the doctor," Mom continued. "I don't like the sound of her cough."

"You'd better get an appointment," agreed Dad.

A busy day got even busier. As Gina washed the dishes, Mom planned. "We'll do the baking first," she said. "Then we'll prepare food to put into the oven when we get home. The cleaning will have to wait for now. We'll see how much time we have left."

"I can clean while you're gone," Gina volunteered.

"Why, so you can." Mom smiled at her. "Dad will be working in the barn, so you can stay here. My, it's nice to have a girl big enough to help like that."

Gina was glad to hear Mom say that. It felt nice to be growing up.

The morning passed swiftly, and by 11:30 a cake was cooling on the counter and a potato casserole and meat loaf were cooling in the refrigerator.

Mom prepared a Jell-O salad while Gina set the table with fixings for sandwiches.

After lunch, Mom gave Gina instructions. "I have to go now if I'm to have Julie at the doctor's office by 2:30. Wash the dishes, Gina. Sweep the kitchen floor and vacuum the carpet after you pick up the stray stuff. Clean the mudroom sink too. The boys' hands must have been very muddy when they washed up, and not all the mud went down the drain. Can you do all this work?"

"Yes," Gina answered confidently. "Is there anything else?"

"Make sure your bedroom is ready for company too. That shouldn't keep you busy all afternoon. You can do what you like after you're done. It could be after four till I get home, though I hope not. Uncle Dan and his family might be here before then."

Gina busied herself with the dishes and finished just as Mom was backing out the driveway.

I did that quickly, Gina thought. *It's not going to take me long at all. It's fun to work by myself.*

She noticed the bowl of garbage on the counter. Mom didn't like that sitting around. She'd better empty it.

The chickens were glad to see her and the garbage. She had fun feeding them the potato peelings one by one. Chickens could be so funny with the way they jerked their heads around, "talking" to themselves all the time. It was several minutes until Gina thought about getting back to work.

She returned to the kitchen and swept the floor. Through the screen door she saw three kittens rolling around on the floor. She had to stop and laugh at the way they tumbled. Surely she could play with them just a little bit. She trailed a bit of string around for them to pounce on.

The kittens seemed extra cute this afternoon as they pounced and snarled. She played with them until they lay down under the bushes to have a nap.

Back to work, she reminded herself. *This is the way I like to work. I don't have to hurry. I can take my time.*

She got the sweeper out. Its busy hum filled the house for a few minutes. Then the sound subsided. Had Dad come into the house at that moment, he would have caught a guilty girl with her nose in a magazine. Minutes passed. More minutes ticked by. The clock hands moved much farther than Gina realized.

Was Gina ever going to look up? Five more minutes passed, and then five more. Finally Gina looked up. Not 3:15 already! She'd have to hurry. Mom would be coming soon.

Quickly she picked up some toys and books scattered around. She had just started sweeping again when a knock sounded on the door.

There was Eva, smiling, and her mom and dad behind her. Gina's smile felt a little stiff as she welcomed her guests, but she managed to say, "Come in. I was just cleaning the floor."

"We heard the sweeper," said Eva. "I had to knock three times."

Gina's mind whirred. *Oh, Eva is here; Eva, whom I love to spend time with. But the floor isn't swept and the sink isn't cleaned. Oh, what is Mom going to say?*

"Mom had to take Julie to the doctor," Gina explained to Aunt Jean. "She hoped to be back before four."

"That's okay. That's okay," said Aunt Jean. "I'll just rest here on the recliner. I got sleepy driving."

Uncle Dan headed for the barn and the smaller children to the sandbox.

Eva said, "Let's go up to your room. Did you change anything since I was here last?"

Gina felt embarrassed when she opened her bedroom door and saw the rumpled bed. Quickly she drew up the covers.

Eva didn't mention the unmade bed. She chattered about her own room and about how they had moved the furniture around. "But it's hard to keep it clean with two little sisters in there," she sighed. "Do you have that problem with Julie?"

"Not too much," admitted Gina. "She keeps her dolls and stuff downstairs in the toy room." Gina glanced around her bedroom. The dress on the floor was hers, and the books and shoes were too. How she wished she had cleaned up everything.

Before long Mom came home. Gina dreaded going downstairs, but she had to sooner or later.

Mom gave her a puzzled look, but all she said was, "Gina, put the sweeper away."

"I'm sorry for coming on such an unsuitable day," Aunt Jean apologized.

"Oh, don't worry about that," replied Mom. "We're glad to see you anytime. And I've got a big girl to help me."

Gina blushed and ducked her head. What was Mom going to say when she saw the dirty sink in the mudroom? Maybe she could go clean it now. Oh, no! It was too late. Aunt Jean was headed there already.

The families talked and talked that evening, enjoying a good time together. Gina joined in too, but she kept remembering that undone work. What was Aunt Jean thinking?

The next morning Mom looked at Gina with a perplexed

look and asked, "Did you clean the sink yesterday?"

Then the whole story tumbled out. Gina told Mom how she had thought she'd have time to do other things and how she hadn't gotten everything done. "You said I was a big help, but I wasn't," she finished.

"It's what I've always said," began Mom.

Gina grinned and said the saying for her: "Work first and then play."

"That's exactly what I was going to say," Mom said in surprise.

"I've known that saying very well for a long time because you always say it, but now I guess I found out for myself how true it is," Gina admitted.

16

The
Treasure Box

Joyce stopped slicing bread when Dad backed through the kitchen door with a large banana box in his arms. She had been enjoying the fragrance of the freshly baked loaves, but now she looked at Dad curiously. What was in that box?

"I got some books at the sale," he said, setting the box on the table with a thud.

"Are they good ones?" asked Mom.

"Should be. I bought them at my cousin's sale. Did you forget?"

"So many books aren't fit to read these days," Mom explained. "I guess I wasn't thinking about whose sale it was." She turned toward Dad but kept stirring the gravy on the stove.

"Here's a commentary I spotted right away on the top," continued Dad, lifting out the book for all to see. "And here's a

Bible dictionary and a Bible atlas. This concordance is smaller than mine and will be easier for the children to use.

"Ah, and here . . ." He raised his eyes and looked at Joyce teasingly. He pretended to peek into the box again, and again raised his eyes to Joyce. "Here are some children's books and youth books too, Joyce."

Joyce went over to see. She peeked into the box and smiled at him. They each knew what the other was thinking. *Books! What a treasure!*

A musty smell hung around the box, but Joyce didn't care. The big box was half filled with children's and youth books. The cover of one book pictured children dressed in old-fashioned clothes. *Black Beauty* was about a horse. There was another one full of stories about animals and another of stories about children around the world. There were missionary stories, a Bible story book with pictures, pioneer stories, and one about a handicapped girl. Since they had never had many story books at their house, this was a box full of treasure.

Joyce wasn't done looking through the books before Mom called, "Joyce, you'll have to put the books back into the box and wipe the table again. They're probably dusty. I have supper ready and Judy needs to get the table set. I hope those books don't keep interfering with your work."

Joyce longed for a closer look, but she hurriedly put the books back into the box. As she wiped the table again and helped get supper on the table, her mind was busy making plans. Those books could last her a long time. She had never before had so many at one time. Some of them were old, but what did that matter? A torn or plain cover on a book didn't spoil the words inside it. Some of the books looked kind of boring, but there were plenty of exciting ones too.

She would read them carefully and finish one before she started another. Oh, what reading enjoyment stretched before her!

Joyce found it hard to leave the books alone. She would think of them longingly every time she went upstairs for something. For a while she was very strict with herself and only read a little when her work was done. Before many days passed, though, she came short of her lofty plans. She was upstairs putting wash away as fast as she could when the thought came, *Why not peek at the next page or two of the book she was reading?* The story was exciting, and page two gave way to three, and three to four . . . The next thing she knew, Mom was standing in the doorway.

"You aren't supposed to be reading, are you, Joyce? If you can't control those books, I'll have to keep them for you and give one to you only when your work is done. You have a little time to read each evening we're home, and longer on Sundays. Surely that's enough."

Joyce certainly didn't want Mom to take the box of books. "I'll do better," she promised.

"I hope so," Mom said, leaving Joyce alone with her thoughts. Her heart sank down to her shoes. Take the books? Mom couldn't do that. It would be harder to get them and would waste precious reading time.

After Mom's threat, Joyce carefully stayed away from the books when she was supposed to be working. She conscientiously followed her own personal goals too. She waded through some books though she found them boring. Others like *Talks with Girls* were good, but she had great difficulty staying interested until she was done with them.

One day her older cousin Lily came to help them do some sewing. Lily liked books too and asked Joyce if she was enjoying that box of books she'd seen Dad buy at the sale.

"Oh, yes," Joyce replied eagerly, and began telling Lily about her favorite ones.

Lily had read most of the books too, and they discussed their favorite parts. Then Joyce mentioned *Talks with Girls*. Lily had never heard of that one. At lunch, Joyce got it and showed it to her, and Lily began skimming through the pages.

"This is one you really do want to read and think about," Lily said. "It has lots of good advice in it."

"I liked it at first," Joyce answered, "but it was too much after a while. I couldn't really take it into my mind like I know I should have, even though I finished it."

"I know exactly what you mean," Lily said, nodding her head. "It's too much information to read in one sitting. Try reading a chapter a day, kind of like a devotional time. If you read a book like this one chapter at a time and then meditate on it, you'll get a lot more out of it. I don't try to finish a book like this before I read another, but it's a good discipline to read a serious book like this along with story books."

Joyce liked Lily's advice. It made her feel better about reading two books at a time. There were two kinds of books to be read in two different ways. For a while, she didn't let reading interfere with her work, but then she again began sneaking bits of time here and there to read. She felt guilty about it, and after a week or two she confessed it to Mom.

"Joyce," her mom said, "I'm glad you told me about your struggles. Just your telling me about them makes me feel I can trust you to handle this situation yourself. I'll talk it over with Dad. He'll probably understand it better than I do."

Joyce was glad she had told Mom. She knew that whatever Dad decided would make good sense because he shared her fascination with books.

Mom was so busy it was rare to see her sit down to talk, but one day she said, "Joyce, let's sit down here at the table for a few minutes to talk." Joyce couldn't bring herself to look into Mom's eyes. What would Mom say? Sitting there, it was easier to look at the wisps of stray hair that always surrounded Mom's face after working hard.

"Joyce," Mom began, "when you told me you how you felt about your reading, I began to realize you are probably mature enough to handle this on your own. I don't need to monitor your reading so closely anymore. I feel like I can trust you."

Wow! Joyce was surprised.

"Dad tried to explain how reading is for him and how he sees it may be for you. Reading has always been the best way for him to learn things. And he says it doesn't always fit into neat hours of 'now is the time to read.' Sometimes, he says, he snatches minutes here and there to read, and then while he works, he thinks about what he read. Later he might snatch a few minutes to reread it to make sure he understood it correctly. Or, he might read on to see what else the author has to say. I do know he always tries to have something with him to read when he might have to wait at the garage or some other place. Many times he is reading a book before or after lunch. Sometimes he doesn't even take the time to sit down to read. But he doesn't let reading interfere with his work."

Joyce knew what her mom was talking about. She had often seen Dad with a book in his hand, yet he always got his work done. She had also noticed what kind of material he was reading.

"Dad is always reading church papers and sermon-type books," she said to Mom. "He doesn't like story books as much as I do. Maybe his reading is better."

Mom smiled an extra big smile. "Joyce, you will be all right with your reading if you keep these good attitudes of wanting to read the right things. Dad said something about that too. He said reading stories at your age is 'milk' for young minds and that later you will grow to appreciate the 'meat' of deeper books and learn to like reading them."

"Oh, Mom," Joyce said, and stopped. What else could she say to a mom who understood her even when she didn't understand her love for reading? They both stood up. Before Mom could leave, Joyce reached out and hugged her hard. Her mom was the best!

17
Annette and a Pair of Shoes

Cindy envied Annette's sureness. Even though she and Annette were about the same height, she made Cindy feel tall and awkward. Annette was ladylike. Her voice was quiet and sweet, and her laughter was like bells. It seemed Annette always knew what to say and do, and everyone admired her.

One day when Mom and Cindy were shopping, Cindy saw shoes that looked almost like the ones Annette had worn to the last youth gathering. Everybody had proclaimed them cute. Cindy showed the shoes to Mom.

"Do you need them?" Mom asked.

"Well, not really," Cindy admitted. "But I can pay for them myself."

"Well, if you're willing to pay for them, you can get them."

Cindy thought for a long time about those shoes. She hardly ever had any money of her own to spend, and it was hard to part with it. Did she really want those shoes? She couldn't decide until Mom said, "Come. I'm ready to go."

Cindy quickly made up her mind and bought the shoes. She wore them at the next youth gathering, hoping someone would compliment her on her new shoes. No one did. The youth finished their games and got up for refreshments. Would someone notice now? Still no one said anything. Finally, she decided to just tuck her feet under her chair. No one noticed her new shoes anyway.

When Cindy got home, she put the shoes in the back of her closet and tried not to think of the book she had hoped to buy with the money she had spent on them.

A few months later, when she had almost forgotten about those shoes, Mom asked, "Why don't you ever wear those shoes you bought?"

Cindy shrugged. "I didn't like them after all."

"But you even spent your own money for them."

Cindy shrugged again.

Mom kept looking at her in a puzzled way.

Cindy tried to explain. "Annette has smaller feet, and the shoes were cute on her. Everyone said so. But on me . . ." She shrugged for the third time. "My feet are so big that no shoes look cute on me. I should have known better. I never did like those kinds of shoes anyway. I've always thought they make my feet look big."

"Uh-huh," Mom answered thoughtfully, and left it with that.

The next day when they were working side by side in the kitchen, Mom brought up the subject again. "I've been thinking about why you bought those shoes. I don't think you need to worry about being like Annette. You are pretty special yourself. God gave you an attractive face, and you have abilities that not everyone has."

"I don't know," Cindy answered honestly. "Martha is always telling me how smart I am. I may be good at books and stuff, but I'd rather be popular." What she added in her thoughts but didn't say was, *I'd rather be popular than pretty too.*

Mom touched Cindy lightly on the shoulder. "Being popular isn't everything. There are popular people who are secretly very sad. One girl I went to youth gatherings with seemed to have everything going for her. Later she confided to me her inferior feelings of being ugly and dumb compared to her sisters."

That was hard to believe. Cindy couldn't imagine Annette ever feeling inferior. It was a puzzle to her. She tried to tell herself she'd never be popular and that it really didn't matter anyway.

Early in the fall Cindy found a use for the "Annette" shoes when Dad said a school board member had asked if she'd be interested in teaching art for the elementary grades at their Christian day school.

Was Cindy interested? She sure was. Excitedly she went to school wearing those shoes. She liked to plan art activities, but it was even more fun sharing them with the children. The children responded enthusiastically. They liked her!

One day she had her head in the supply cupboard, putting colored paper, glue, strings, pompoms, and other items in their proper places. School was out for the day, but she could hear Sister Susie talking to a child in the adjoining classroom.

The child's voice was distraught and laced with tears. Susie's tone was smooth and comforting. Cindy could easily picture them together: the child in her desk and Susie right beside her in another. Susie's petite figure wasn't much bigger than the children she taught. She often slid into the seats beside them—after hours, that is. She could be a drill sergeant too when the occasion required.

Susie was several years older than Cindy, but Cindy sometimes felt more comfortable talking to her than to most of her own age group. Some of this was because of their shared love for teaching.

The child was talking again. Then Cindy heard Susie's words. "I'm sure the other girls like you," she comforted. "I'd like for you to try something. Say 'Hi' to the other children when you get to school. You don't have to say it to everybody, but to the people near you. And don't forget to smile. People like cheerful people. Do you think you could do that?" She paused a minute.

Then Cindy heard Susie's voice again. "Be careful to always say kind things. When you go home, tell your friends goodbye."

Cindy was listening with all her might. She didn't want to miss a word. When Susie gave that last advice, Cindy remembered the little chorus of "See ya's" that had always accompanied leaving school and how she'd often felt left out because no one said "See ya" to her. Foolish, it seemed now.

"Sometimes you have to talk to your friends instead of waiting around for them to talk to you." Susie was counseling now.

That was something Cindy was afraid to do. She almost always waited for someone to talk to her, and often she may as well have been the wallpaper for all the notice she got.

"I know sometimes it's hard to know what to say, but start with something small. Say something like, 'Are you going to do anything special tonight?' Or, 'Did you like art class?' " Then Susie's voice faded. Soon Cindy heard the door open and close.

When she felt it safe to leave her hidden spot, she peeked into Susie's classroom. She saw Susie's blonde head bent over papers on her desk and felt it was okay to enter.

"Oh!" Susie looked up startled. "Are you still here? I thought everyone had gone."

"No," Cindy said, "you had two listeners to your sage advice."

"Oh, that. I didn't know you were listening. I think I give that same advice every year. Friends are so important to children."

"And not to you?" Cindy couldn't keep herself from asking.

"Oh, well, yes, to me too. Of course I need friends. In fact, I think that's why I so often give 'friend' advice. It's been something I've had to work at all my life even though I gave up being popular years ago. I've learned to be content with enjoying my work and having friends." She smiled a tiny rueful smile.

"I am at the right school then." Cindy smiled a big, happy smile at her. "I need a lot of teaching on that very subject. I am so dumb at things like that. What you've said today suddenly makes having friends seem a lot simpler. And that's really what I want too. I don't need to be popular either."

That was a lot for Cindy to say as she shared her own struggles. She suddenly blushed and felt herself folding up in embarrassment.

Susie simply smiled again and gave her a little wave as Cindy ducked out of the classroom.

When Cindy was out of sight, she shook her head. For her, the art of being friendly wasn't going to happen in a day, but now it looked simpler. Susie's advice had given her a place to start. *It makes a lot more sense than wearing shoes like someone else's,* she thought, looking ruefully at the disliked ones on her feet.

18

Only for Fun

Debbie's eyes met Joe's as they laughed at the teacher's funny story. Joe's grin showed even teeth in his tanned face. Seeing that grin turned her way was fun, and Debbie began to think about it happening again. One day she overheard Joe talking to his friend by the lockers.

"We scared him so bad he couldn't get out of there fast enough. That was the first we knew he could run." The boys laughed.

Debbie laughed too, even though she had not heard the whole story. The two boys turned, and for the first time Debbie noticed Luke's eyes looking at her curiously. It would be fun to have those eyes looking at her again.

The next day she passed several students and teachers on the stairs, but she didn't say anything to anyone until Luke passed. "Hello, Luke," she caroled, and was rewarded with a glance from his eyes and a slight upturning of his lips.

More and more opportunities seemed to come up to have fun with Joe and Luke. Often Tom was with them too. He was a good joker who liked to make her laugh. Joking with him was fun too.

These encounters made school more exciting than just studying math, history, and the other subjects. Class time became a time to enjoy the boys more than to listen to the teacher.

Debbie had been having a good time like this for a few weeks when Mom spoke up.

"Debbie," she said as they were working side by side, Debbie rolling out pie crust while Mom peeled the apples, "I'm wondering if you're not too friendly with the boys at school."

Debbie felt color coming into her cheeks. She didn't know how to answer and kept her eyes on the rolling pin as she lifted it up and smoothed out the pie crust again.

"When I wait to pick up the school children, I watch all of you high schoolers come out. It seems you are almost always laughing and chatting with a boy or two. Is this what happens all day?"

Debbie shrugged. "We are only talking and having fun."

"At your age, boys and girls sometimes begin to notice each other in a different way than before," Mom continued. "This is normal because God has created in each of us a desire to marry, but for you, that is still many years in the future. For now you need to work hard at schoolwork and have girlfriends for your closest friends."

Debbie shrugged again. "I do have girlfriends, but boys are more fun sometimes. It is more fun to joke with them."

"Debbie, look at me." Mom's voice was stern.

Debbie look up to see Mom's grave face. It made Debbie feel guilty, yet she wondered what was wrong with a little fun.

Mom went on. "Do you think Dad would be pleased if I talked and laughed with other men? Do you think that would be right?"

Debbie shrugged again and lowered her gaze to Mom's shoes. Somehow that felt more comfortable than looking at Mom's face.

"God's plan is for one man and one woman to be only for each other in marriage. You know that. This talking and laughing with all the boys is not good even though you won't be married for a long time. It is not pleasing to God. This is called flirting, and it is wrong."

Deep in her heart, Debbie knew Mom was right, but flirting was fun. What could it hurt if she did it only at school with boys she knew? They all knew none of them would be dating for a long time.

The next day at school she snatched Joe's pencil from his desk when she walked by. She felt a twinge of guilt, knowing what Mom had said, but she was going to have her fun anyway. A new boldness crept into her heart, and the new daring felt exciting.

Joe noticed his missing pencil. He looked behind his books and on the floor. Not finding it, he blurted, "Hey, who took my pencil?"

No one answered. A few snickers escaped from classmates. He looked around and noticed Debbie studiously looking at a paper. The pencil showed innocently in her hand.

"Hey," he said again and dived for the pencil, reaching over her desk as she mischievously withdrew it from his reach.

"Students," Teacher Vernon called out, "what is going on?"

Debbie meekly gave up the pencil, and Joe retreated to his seat with it in his hand.

"All of you sit down," said the teacher. "Joe, I would like to see you in my office when I dismiss the class for break."

Joe had his turn in the office, and then it was Debbie's turn.

"Can you tell me what part you had in the ruckus this morning before we started?" asked Teacher Vernon.

"I just took Joe's pencil for a joke," said Debbie in a small voice as she studied the shiny surface of the principal's desk.

"Is there a reason you chose Joe's pencil?" He paused briefly and then went on without waiting for an answer. "I've noticed your extra friendliness to Joe and a couple of other boys too. All of you come to school to learn. It isn't a place to find girlfriends and boyfriends. You shouldn't be giving special attention to any boy. Sure, you may be friendly to the boys, but give more attention to girls for your friendship needs."

He paused again and studied the desktop. Then he turned to her and asked, "Have you heard of any of this before?"

"Yes," Debbie meekly answered.

"What are you going to do about it?"

Debbie shrugged.

"Here's my plan," Teacher Vernon said. "I expect to see you give more attention to your schoolwork and no special attention to the boys. Can you do that?"

Debbie answered in a small voice, "I'll try." But as she left the office, she thought, *I'll just have to be more careful for a while.* She tried to ignore her conscience, which accused her of telling a lie.

Debbie became more careful in her teacher's presence, and she remembered that Mom was watching as she walked out at dismissal time. She found other times to make Joe show his grin, and Luke to turn his eyes on her. She even exchanged a few witty remarks with Tom.

Sam was in a younger grade and seemed like a little boy, but soon even he became fun to tease. She would tell him things to upset him because he got worked up so quickly.

Feeling quite successful in hiding all of this for about a month, she headed down the stairs to the basement one day. Suddenly she heard boys' voices . . . then her name. She stopped to remain hidden and see if she could hear more.

"That's the way Debbie is," said Joe. "She's a flirt."

"I know," answered Luke. "Sometimes I just wish she'd mind her own business."

Tom's voice was serious for once and sounded lower than normal. Debbie didn't recognize it at first. "It's just boys, boys, boys in her mind," he said. "Have you noticed how she even carries on with Sam now? It's getting disgusting. Ruth says she hardly talks to any girls at all."

Debbie's ears burned. She had to get out of there, but before she did, she heard Joe add, "I'd never want her for a girlfriend. Who'd want a girlfriend who flirts with everyone else?"

Debbie turned and fled up the stairs. She dashed into

the girls' room where she could have a few moments of privacy. Oh, what hot shame filled her heart! What had she done? What was she going to do now? How would she face everyone again? If only she had listened to Mom!

Embarrassed or not, Debbie had to return to class. She listened carefully to everything her teacher said and stayed at her desk reading her literature book when the rest of the class took their break. She became one of the most studious students for the rest of the school year. Sometimes one of the boys bumped her elbow or her book as they passed, but she ignored their efforts to get her attention. Never again would she make a fool of herself by flirting.

19
It's the Love That Matters

Ruth was seventeen and her sister Betty was thirteen. Having a little sister thrilled Ruth at first, but as Betty grew up, Ruth changed her mind. If her parents were stricter with Betty, things would go better. They babied her so. Ruth was sure she would never have gotten by with the things Betty did.

Ruth thought Betty would do better after she became a Christian that spring. Betty did read her Bible and pray, but some of the things she did sure didn't seem very Christian. She couldn't keep her room clean and she lost lots of things. One day she came over into Ruth's room to ask to borrow her comb.

"Why don't you use your own comb?" Ruth asked.

"I can't find it."

"It's no wonder you can't find it," Ruth retorted. "I'd lose my stuff too if I left my things lying around on the floor like you do."

"I do try to keep my room clean," Betty replied in a small voice. "May I borrow your comb just this once?"

"I'll find it for you," Ruth announced, and marched into her room. "Here it is," she soon called. "It was in this pile of pictures and junk. Why don't you clean up this mess anyway?"

"That's my scrapbooking stuff," Betty explained. "I'm making a scrapbook for Sally. I left it out because I'm not done."

"I've heard that story before," Ruth snapped. "You're always making cards or a scrapbook for someone, and this stuff is never put away."

Later Ruth said the same thing to Mom, who answered, "Is that so terrible? I think it's wonderful the way she thinks of others and cheers them up."

"But she should clean it up," Ruth insisted.

"I'll let her decide about that," Mom said more decidedly. "If she wants to keep it out until the project is done, I don't mind. If it ends up cluttering her room too long, though, I'll remind her to put it away. I know she will do what I ask without complaining."

Maybe Mom didn't think scrapbooking messes had anything to do with being a Christian, but there were other things Betty did too. She was always telling the dumbest jokes, and sometimes she seemed to laugh just for the sake of laughing. Weren't Christians supposed to be serious instead of silly?

And then she teased little children. Ruth didn't think it was kind, but Mom just said, "They all love her, don't they?"

"Yes, I guess they do love her," admitted Ruth.

"She's a lot younger than you and has a lot of growing up

to do," Mom reminded Ruth. "You can't expect her to be perfect, can you? None of us is perfect."

"But we need to help her try," Ruth insisted.

"She is trying," answered Mom. "I think you need to remember she is several years younger than you. She is a Christian and loves the Lord. She is learning and growing all the time. We all are. You are farther along the road of life than she is.

"Think of her as a rosebud, beautiful and perfect in its own way, though not yet in full bloom. You, at seventeen, are opening up into a rose because you are older. Her thirteen-year-old heart wants to serve God, and she loves others. She is a beautiful rosebud."

Ruth didn't answer Mom aloud, but inwardly she felt frustrated that her mom made so many excuses for Betty.

———

That fall Ruth had to spend a few days in the hospital and was the "lucky" recipient of one of those homemade cards. Betty handed it to Ruth with a big smile.

"Thanks," Ruth said as politely as she could. She opened the envelope. A large flower with many petals graced the cover of the card.

It would have taken some time to cut and glue all those petals, Ruth thought begrudgingly. She studied it a minute and opened the card. Inside Betty had written "Cast all your cares upon Him, for He careth for you." The lettering was neat, but she had forgotten the "e" in "careth."

Ruth looked at the front again and spotted the glue that held the center of the flower. She scratched it with her fingernail to see if she could get it off.

"Don't scratch it," Betty pleaded.

"But there's glue here," Ruth replied. "And inside you forgot the 'e' in 'careth.' "

Everyone in the room became quiet, and Betty got up to leave. When Ruth looked up, all she saw of her sister's retreating figure was the fuzzy hair on her hanging head.

"Ruth," Dad spoke sternly, "that wasn't kind."

"But she's thirteen, and if she's going to give things like this to people, she needs to learn to do it right," Ruth insisted. "I'm only speaking the truth in love."

"Ruth, there was no love at all in what you said," Dad returned. "You were critical, and you didn't even express appreciation for the time she put into the card. That was her love. You didn't see the sparkle in her eye and the smile on her face. That was her love. Her cards don't have to be perfect to communicate love."

He studied Ruth a minute, but she refused to meet his eyes. She kept her eyes on the card and thought stubbornly, *They treat Betty like a baby. It's time she grows up.*

When Ruth came home from the hospital, she had a different little sister. Betty cleaned up her messes now, but her brown eyes didn't sparkle at Ruth anymore. She was quiet and hardly ever joked. A small smile had replaced her gay laugh. Ruth missed her coming into her room to borrow her comb.

Ruth tried teasing her. She tried asking for one of her homemade cards to give to a friend. She bought Betty her favorite candy. Nothing worked.

Finally Ruth apologized. "Sorry, Betty, for being mean to you."

Betty's eyes studied Ruth seriously for several seconds. Finally she managed to say, "Don't worry about it," and turned to walk quietly away.

In a way, Ruth had done what she had wanted to do: she had "grown her little sister up." But as time went on, she regretted more than ever her rude actions and the "little sister" she had lost through it.

Several years went by before Betty made cards again. Then she painted gorgeous scenery with water colors and wrote verses in calligraphy. She threw away any cards that she thought had slight imperfections.

Ruth said, "Don't throw them out. They're beautiful. I don't even notice the mistakes. And what Dad said is true. It is the love that matters."

But Betty stubbornly said, "I have to learn to make them right."

Oh, not anymore, Ruth's heart cried silently. *You've learned to make them so beautifully. It's the open, loving heart that isn't there anymore.*

"Betty," Ruth said fervently, "the love is more important. It's the love that makes people happy when you give them your cards." It must have been the anguish in Ruth's voice that made Betty study her with astonished eyes.

"But you're the one who said I need to make them right," she said.

"I was wrong. I was wrong," repeated Ruth. "It's the love.

Didn't Paul say that great things like prophecy, knowledge, and faith to move mountains mean nothing if there is no love?"

"But if I take the time to make them perfectly, that shows my love," said Betty.

"No, no, no," insisted Ruth. "Love will work carefully, but I was wrong when I spoke to you so unkindly. When you were learning, sure there were going to be a few mistakes. There may even be mistakes now, but that is okay. Your love is shown by the time and effort you put into making a card, even if the card isn't perfect. It is the thought. It is the smile. That is the love."

"Okay," said Betty. "I like that. I really do. I love to give away love." Her eyes twinkled, and Ruth saw a glimpse of the happy heart of her little sister again.

> And though I have the gift of prophecy, and understand all mysteries, and all knowledge; and though I have all faith, so that I could remove mountains, and have not charity, I am nothing.
> 1 Corinthians 13:2

20

Against the Darkness

Over the years I've forgotten many of my classrooms, but there is one I remember very well from my junior high years because of what happened there one afternoon in the early 70s.

The inner wall of the classroom that I remember so well was made mostly of windows. Through the glass we could look into a courtyard in the middle of the public schoolhouse. As far as we knew, this oasis of green was just to rest our eyes; no one ever went in there. A large blackboard covered the front wall of our classroom, and a doorway to our right opened to the hallway. A bulletin board hung to the right of the doorway.

Our teacher's large, gray metal desk was in the front of the room. The students' desks were gray metal too, with wooden tops. Each desk had a shelf underneath for books, but most of our books were kept in hall lockers that we opened with individual number combinations.

Mrs. R., was a married woman, barely middle-aged, and of average height. Her straight brown hair were cut rather short, and she wore little makeup or jewelry. Her clothes were "teacher" clothes, not outstanding in any way. She was an ordinary teacher with calm, polite, kind ways.

I enjoyed Mrs. R.'s literature class. Sometimes we used a textbook and sometimes she passed out copies of a paperback book for us to read and discuss together. The students were surprisingly co-operative and participated well in our many discussions. I learned about new stories, poems, and books in her class, and I don't remember any of it being offensive.

I do remember a long epic poem I chose to read and report orally on. Getting an A on this oral report was enough to make it stick in my memory. But that's not the reason I remember this classroom so well.

The day before the notorious event, Mrs. R. had been talking to some of the students informally after the last class. Knowing she often spent extra time talking to certain students, I wouldn't have given it much thought, but on this particular day the discussion seemed to be in earnest.

The next day an expectant air hung over the classroom. I heard excited whispers. Something new was in the classroom, but I didn't know what it was. A group of students had huddled around something.

"Close the door," someone whispered.

"Ouija board," I next heard whispered around the room. I had never seen an Ouija board, but I had heard of it. It was a board with a needle that was fastened yet free to move. People placed their hands on the board and asked it questions.

Supposedly the needle would move of its own accord to answer yes or no.

I wasn't going to get any closer to see. I knew enough about this board to know the needle moved by an unseen evil power. Some students crowded around the board. Others stayed in their seats like I did.

Mrs. R. walked over to the classroom door and looked into the hall through a small glass window set in the top. My uneasiness grew. She remained standing near the door and talked to the class in a low voice.

"Do you know how to use this?" she asked.

"Yes, we do," someone assured her. More students clustered around the board. When everyone seemed settled, she said quietly, "Now someone ask a question."

I don't remember what the question was, but I do know it was a simple question like "Is it raining?"

Everyone waited in breathtaking silence.

"It's not moving," someone whispered.

"Ask it another question," Mrs. R. suggested softly.

After another question and some more silence, someone reported, "It's still not moving."

"Let someone else try," Mrs. R. suggested next.

Some of the students traded seats. Again we waited. "It still won't move," they said.

Mrs. R. asked, "Are your hands flat on it?"

"Yes," they said.

Mrs. R. paused a minute. We all continued to wait. Finally she said, "Is there someone here who doesn't believe in this?"

She didn't look in my direction, but I figured she was

thinking of me. My clothes told her I was a Mennonite. I was the only "plain" student in that room.

My breath stopped for a few seconds. Did I believe it wouldn't work? I believed it could work, but I also believed satanic power made it work.

Mrs. R. spoke again. "If anyone here doesn't believe in this, would you leave the room and stand in the hall?" She kept her eyes averted from me but swept them over the rest of the classroom.

I sat still. My heart pounded *thump, thump, thump* in my ears. What should I do? Should I leave and let them see if the needle would work then? If Satan would work the needle after I left, it didn't seem like a good thing to move. I began to pray silently, *Dear Lord, don't let it work for them.*

More minutes passed. The teacher gave up and that thing was put away. I don't remember what happened after that; I was too busy thinking. Did my presence keep that Ouija board from working? I didn't know for sure, but I knew for certain God that kept that Ouija board from working, and I was glad He did.

Even though many children today go to Christian schools and don't expect anything like this to happen there, Satan hasn't quit working to get young people entangled in his web. White magic, which is popular in books and movies, is of the devil. There is no good witchcraft. Chanting spells to get things accomplished and fortune telling may seem innocent and fun, but dabbling in any of these things gives Satan power over lives.

Powers of darkness are stronger than we are. To be victorious, we need to be strong in the Lord. We need to put on God's armor and be skilled in the use of His Sword (Ephesians 6:10–18). Praise God that His power is greater than the devil's!

> Regard not them that have familiar spirits,
> neither seek after wizards, to be defiled by them:
> I am the LORD your God. Leviticus 19:31

About the Author

Christine Diller and her husband Daryl live in Pennsylvania. Daryl has pastored Burns Valley Mennonite Church for twenty-two years. They have nine children, four sons-in-law, one daughter-in-law, and eleven grandchildren. Christine's desire is to love the Lord with all her heart, soul, and mind. She considers being a wife and mother her highest calling.

Raised by parents who enjoyed reading and who provided good books for their family, Christine became an avid reader early in life. With her father's encouragement, she began writing at the age of fifteen. She wants everything she has written to bring honor and glory to God, trusting that He will shine through her "earthen vessel" in spite of her mistakes.

If you wish to contact the author, you may write to her in care of Christian Aid Ministries, P.O. Box 360, Berlin, Ohio 44610.

About Christian Aid Ministries

Christian Aid Ministries was founded in 1981 as a nonprofit, tax-exempt 501(c)(3) organization. Its primary purpose is to provide a trustworthy and efficient channel for Amish, Mennonite, and other conservative Anabaptist groups and individuals to minister to physical and spiritual needs around the world. This is in response to the command to ". . . do good unto all men, especially unto them who are of the household of faith" (Galatians 6:10).

Each year, CAM supporters provide 15-20 million pounds of food, clothing, medicines, seeds, Bibles, Bible story books, and other Christian literature for needy people. Most of the aid goes to orphans and Christian families. Supporters' funds also help to clean up and rebuild for natural disaster victims, put up Gospel billboards in the U.S., support several church-planting efforts, operate two medical clinics, and provide resources for needy families to make their own living. CAM's main purposes for providing aid are to help and encourage God's people and bring the Gospel to a lost and dying world.

CAM has staff, warehouses, and distribution networks in Romania, Moldova, Ukraine, Haiti, Nicaragua, Liberia, Israel, and Kenya. Aside from management, supervisory personnel, and bookkeeping operations, volunteers do most of the work at CAM locations. Each year, volunteers at our warehouses, field bases, Disaster Response Services projects, and other locations donate over 200,000 hours of work.

CAM's ultimate purpose is to glorify God and help enlarge His kingdom. ". . . whatsoever ye do, do all to the glory of God" (1 Corinthians 10:31).

The Way to God and Peace

We live in a world contaminated by sin. Sin is anything that goes against God's holy standards. When we do not follow the guidelines that God our Creator gave us, we are guilty of sin. Sin separates us from God, the source of life.

Since the time when the first man and woman, Adam and Eve, sinned in the Garden of Eden, sin has been universal. The Bible says that we all have "sinned and come short of the glory of God" (Romans 3:23). It also says that the natural consequence for that sin is eternal death, or punishment in an eternal hell: "Then when lust hath conceived, it bringeth forth sin: and sin, when it is finished, bringeth forth death" (James 1:15).

But we do not have to suffer eternal death in hell. God provided a sacrifice for our sins through the gift of His only Son, Jesus Christ. "For God so loved the world that he gave his only begotten Son, that whosoever believeth in him should not perish, but have everlasting life" (John 3:16).

A sacrifice is something given to benefit someone else. It costs the giver greatly. Jesus was God's sacrifice. Jesus' death takes away the penalty of sin for all those who accept this sacrifice and truly repent of their sins. To repent of sins means to be truly sorry for and turn away from the things we have done that have violated God's standards (Acts 2:38; 3:19).

Jesus died, but He did not remain dead. After three days, God's Spirit miraculously raised Him to life again. God's Spirit does something similar in us. When we receive Jesus as our sacrifice and repent of our sins, our hearts are changed. We become spiritually alive! We develop new desires and attitudes (2 Corinthians 5:17). We begin to make choices that please God (1 John 3:9). If we do fail and commit sins, we can ask God for forgiveness. "If we confess our sins, he is faithful and just to forgive us our sins, and to cleanse us from all unrighteousness" (1 John 1:9).

Once our hearts have been changed, we want to continue growing spiritually. We will be happy to let Jesus be the Master of our lives and will want to become more like Him. To do this, we must meditate on God's Word and commune with God in prayer. We will testify to others of this change by being baptized and sharing the good news of God's victory over sin and death. Fellowship with a faithful group of believers will strengthen our walk with God (1 John 1:7).